The Art of Communication
in a Polarized World

The
Art of
Communication
in a
Polarized
World

KYLE CONWAY

◊ AU PRESS

Published by AU Press, Athabasca University
1200, 10011 – 109 Street, Edmonton, AB T5J 3S8
https://doi.org/10.15215/aupress/9781771992930.01

Cover image © Suchat Nuchpleng / Shutterstock.com
Cover design by Natalie Olsen
Interior design by Sergiy Kozakov
Printed and bound in Canada

Library and Archives Canada Cataloguing in Publication

Title: The art of communication in a polarized world / Kyle Conway.
Names: Conway, Kyle, 1977- author.
Description: Includes bibliographical references and index.
Identifiers: Canadiana (print) 20200162683 | Canadiana (ebook) 20200162691
        ISBN 9781771992930 (softcover) | ISBN 9781771992947 (pdf)
        ISBN 9781771992954 (epub) | ISBN 9781771992961 (Kindle)
Subjects: LCSH: Intercultural communication. | LCSH: Translating and interpreting.
        LCSH: Communication and culture. | LCSH: Language and culture.
Classification: LCC P94.6 C66 2020 | DDC 303.48/2—dc23

This book has been published with the help of a grant from the Federation
for the Humanities and Social Sciences, through the Awards to Scholarly
Publications Program, using funds provided by the Social Sciences and
Humanities Research Council of Canada.

We acknowledge the financial support of the Government of Canada through
the Canada Book Fund (CBF) for our publishing activities and the assistance
provided by the Government of Alberta through the Alberta Media Fund.

Canadä   Albertan
                Government

For K., my compass
For E. and B., world-changers

Contents

Figures

Preface

What This Book Is, and What It Isn't

———•———

This book is part of an answer to a question I asked when I was redesigning a course I often teach: how might a class, taken as a unit of which a book is merely part, serve as a vehicle for ideas? I was thinking about how different types of writing express ideas differently. A song, a novel, and a comic book can all recount the same events, but they won't tell the same story. Likewise, a monograph, an article, and a conference paper can all report the same results, but they won't convey the same ideas. So how might a class—with its books, its syllabus, its assignments, its regularly scheduled meetings, its questions and answers—become a collective, collaborative text? Who could read it? What would they learn?[1]

I wrote this book with these questions in mind. It's a trace left by the course, so to speak—an echo that gives some sense of what my conversation with my students sounded like. As a result, the chapters that follow might sound like lectures or, if I'm doing things right, turns taken in that conversation. That's by design, in that I use this book to demonstrate the ideas I describe. In the introduction, for instance, I give an example of two people trying to come to a shared

---

1 I've long admired the students of Ferdinand de Saussure, the Swiss linguist whose *Cours de linguistique générale* (1916; published in English in 1959 as *Course in General Linguistics*) laid the foundation for structuralism. He didn't write the book himself. His students did, based on their notes from the course. His clarity and their dedication showed what a course, taken as a unit, might be.

understanding of an object through a series of back-and-forth questions. I engage in similar exchanges throughout this book. The things I want to understand better are communication theory and cultural translation, and those are the things we talk about in class.

Consequently, my first audience has been the students in the course I was redesigning—a third-year undergraduate course on communication theory at the University of Ottawa. They have been worthy partners in conversation. They are smart people, capable of careful and rigorous thought, if they're so inclined. They're willing to work, although like anyone else, they object to work that serves no clear purpose. The most meaningful difference between them and me is that I've had twenty more years to spend reading: when I make references they do not catch, it is not because I'm smarter but because I'm older. These things—my students' intelligence and work ethic on the one hand, and the disparity in our respective levels of experience on the other—explain two choices I've made in the pages that follow. First, I've explained every reference I think even ten students (out of a class of a hundred) might not catch. I've also glossed technical terms they might not have encountered before. Second, I've used pictures wherever they are useful for cutting through the abstractions to which I'm prone, and to which the subject matter lends itself, especially in cases of metacognition and metatheory (thinking about thinking and theory about theory). I want this book to demonstrate that clarity and rigour go hand in hand, a lesson for which I have my students to thank.

So is this book a textbook? Not in a conventional sense. Typical theory textbooks are secondary sources in that they present concepts others have developed, along with explanations of context and explications of ideas. Perhaps the best in this genre is *Theorizing Communication: Readings Across Traditions,* by Robert Craig and Heidi Muller, who organize communication theory into seven such traditions. They reproduce original articles and book chapters to give students more or less direct access to the original expression of each tradition's ideas. But their contribution—what makes their book a textbook—is the work they have done to organize, summarize, and contextualize the readings. In other words, it's a secondary source.

This book approaches theory differently. When I teach, I want to do more than give students a set of ideas to memorize.[2] I want to engage them in the process of *doing* theory—of approaching a question the way a scholar would approach it. In my experience, that means responding to, arguing with, and refining ideas other scholars have proposed. The end result is a new set of ideas. The point of this book is to walk students through these steps—to teach by doing. My model has been the books published for the Open University in England in the 1990s, such as *Doing Cultural Studies: The Story of the Sony Walkman* and *Representation: Cultural Representations and Signifying Practices*.[3] Although they were intended as textbooks, adopting a familiar tone and focusing on the building blocks of theory, they are also about the praxis of teaching. They are shaped by a productive tension between pedagogy and originality: because they demonstrate how to think like a scholar and how to produce new ideas, they must be original themselves. In the same way, the exercise I undertake here is meaningful only if I've written a book other scholars will engage with as a primary source, which is to say, a book that offers a novel take on long-standing questions.

Thus my second audience has been other scholars (but just as this book is not a conventional textbook, it's not a conventional monograph, either). I address two groups explicitly: those in communication and cultural studies and those in translation studies, as I write in the introductory chapter. They will already have read the theorists with whose ideas I engage. They will also recognize the

2 The same is true of Craig and Muller, I'm sure, but whenever I use their textbook, that seems to be what my students expect to do—despite my efforts to the contrary—as soon as they see a list of traditions and their respective readings.

3 Paul du Gay, Stuart Hall, Linda Janes, Hugh Mackay, and Keith Negus, *Doing Cultural Studies: The Story of the Sony Walkman*; and Stuart Hall, ed., *Representation: Cultural Representations and Signifying Practices*.

debates into which I enter, even when I don't name them explicitly. I hope they will take this book on the merits of the arguments it presents, although I also hope they will recognize the way my pedagogical goals shape the presentation of my ideas. If I were writing only for them, I would pursue the implications of certain assertions further, whereas here, I see value in showing students the way arguments work without plunging in to the morass of details that come about when people trained to split hairs go about the business of, well, splitting hairs. For people learning the skills of doing theory, it's enough to read Stuart Hall's "Encoding/Decoding" (as I do in chapter 1) without also having read David Morley's application of the essay in the 1980s, as well as recent revisions of Morley's application of Hall's ideas, and so on.[4] My students are smart—they are more than capable of doing theory—but they don't yet have the background to sort through those details. In fact, the point of this book is to give them the skills to acquire that background.

I am responding to a third group, too, namely philosophers of education whose books have influenced the way I think about teaching. I do not address them explicitly. Instead, this book (and the class of which it is part) is itself my response to their work. In particular, I am guided by the idea that

> it is time to put what is good in the world—that which is under threat and which we wish to preserve—at the centre of our attention and to make a conceptual space in which we can take up our responsibility . . . in the face of, and in spite of, oppression and silent melancholy.[5]

4 David Morley, *The "Nationwide" Audience: Structure and Decoding*; and Sujeong Kim, "Rereading David Morley's The 'Nationwide' Audience." I've adapted this example from Jonathan Culler's *Literary Theory: A Very Short Introduction*.

5 Naomi Hodgson, Joris Vlieghe, and Piotr Zamojski, *Manifesto for a Post-Critical Pedagogy*, 19. Other books to which I am responding are Samuel Rocha's *Folk Phenomenology: Education, Study, and the Human Person* and *A Primer for Philosophy and Education* and, in a very different vein, William Caraher, Kostis Kourelis, and Andrew Reinhard's *Punk Archaeology*.

I like these philosophers because they issue a call to action. ("The philosophers have only interpreted the world, in various ways," wrote Marx in 1845; "the point is to change it.")[6] I'm responding by heeding their call and trying to put their ideas (and mine) into practice. They insist—and I agree—that teaching matters. It matters because thinking matters, and thinking matters because the world is a mysterious place worth exploring and fighting for.

So what is this book? Neither conventional textbook nor conventional monograph, it is a book for thinking with. To complement it (and complete the class-as-text of which it's part), I've included a version of my syllabus in the appendix. This book is meaningful only if people take their turn in the conversation.

With that, let's jump in.

---

6 Karl Marx, "Theses on Feuerbach," thesis XI.

Acknowledgements

·———·

Thank you to my partners in the conversations that became the soil out of which this book grew. Of these, most important have been my students. At the University of North Dakota, where I started my career, I began developing these ideas in Comm 405: Social Implications of an Information Society, and Comm 501: Theoretical Perspectives in Communication. At the University of Ottawa, where I have taught for the past five years, I developed them in CMN 3109: Advanced Theories of Communication, CMN 5132: Theories and Effects of the Media, and CMN 8111: Theories in Media Studies. I am especially indebted to the students in CMN 3109 during the Winter and Spring/Summer 2018 terms and in CMN 5132 and CMN 8111 during the Fall 2018 term, who read and engaged with drafts of different chapters. I am also grateful to the doctoral students at the Universität Trier for their perceptive engagement when I delivered talks based on chapters 2 and 3 as part of the university's IRTG: Diversity program in July 2019.

Going back further, I want to thank my teachers who prized rigour, clarity, and, above all, θαυμάζειν, or *thaumazein*, the sense of astonishment (according to Aristotle) out of which philosophy springs. They include my grade 5 teacher, Mrs. Sprague, Timberwilde Elementary; Mrs. Lorenzetti, my English teacher in grade 8 at Baker Junior High School; Mr. Kornegay, who taught me calculus in grade 11 at Albuquerque High School; and Ms. Parris, my grade 12 English teacher at Albuquerque High School. They also include two of my professors at the University of North Dakota, Kathleen Dixon and Michael Beard, both in the Department of English. Others have been teachers in practice, if not in title, including Brent Christianson, in Madison, Wisconsin, and Erin Burns, in Ottawa. And some are simply my friends, in particular Sam Rocha.

In a narrower sense, I owe a professional debt to Elizabeth Galewski, Joshua Young, and Brett Ommen. If I know anything about rhetorical invention, it is because of them. (But if I can't get my facts straight, that's on me.) Liz, with whom I had coffee once a week when we were students at the University of Wisconsin, taught me about tropological invention and the pleasures of irony. Josh, whose doctoral work I had the privilege of supervising in its final stages, taught me to look for invention in unexpected places. And Brett—he was my colleague and friend at the University of North Dakota. We have since gone our separate ways, but one thing (among many) he showed me was that we can pick and choose what we need from the tools of theory to solve the problem at hand. His approach to theory was endlessly inventive.

In a more immediate sense, I want to thank Enrique Uribe-Jongbloed, now at the Universidad Externado de Colombia, and Craig Walker, at Queen's University. In 2016, Enrique invited me to give the keynote address at a conference on cultural transduction (his term for cultural translation, more or less). That talk became chapter 1 of this book. But the other chapters came from the page of notes I jotted down while listening to Craig's presentation on Petr Pavlenskii. He is no doubt unaware of the way his talk struck me, not only for what he was saying but for what he was *doing*: he made me walk around a concept I thought I knew well (cultural translation) and see it from a new angle.

I also want to thank everyone at Athabasca University Press, especially Pamela Holway. This is an odd book—no two ways around it!—and she was its strongest supporter from the moment I contacted her. I had given myself over to writing it, asking only one thing of each sentence and each idea: *must this be said, and must it be said this way?* It's risky to draw stick figures in an academic book, but Pamela embraced not just the arguments and ideas but also the spirit of the act that created them. I also want to thank the press's director Megan Hall for her enthusiasm, and editor Peter Midgley for his generous and sensitive revisions.

Finally, as always, thank you to Kristi and to Ben and Ellie.

The

Art of

Communication

in a

Polarized

World

Introduction

People's Minds Are Hard to Change

•————————•

People's minds are hard to change. When we encounter a new idea, we compare it to things in the world we already know, and that world—the one we navigate through every day—already makes sense. It is fully formed, and even if an outside viewer might say it's faulty, it seems complete to us. There are no loose ends, and new ideas clash with its completeness. To make sense of them, we ask whether they fit in the world we know, but because they're new, they might not. The problem isn't the new idea—it's the persuasiveness of the world we have come to know and take for granted.[1]

This book is about how to change people's minds. It takes as its starting point two related observations. First, in our modern world, we are faced with tremendous challenges—intense social and political polarization, the looming threat of terror, and the reality of systemic discrimination, to name only a few. Second, these challenges have at

---

1 Many of my students—my first audience in this book—will probably experience this challenge as they read this book. What I want to do is introduce ideas that currently have no place in their symbolic universe. They might not make sense, at least not right now, but I hope that by drawing attention to the challenge itself, I might help my students take a critical step back to see their presuppositions in a new light. This is not an easy task.

For the background literature on this phenomenon, see Janice A. Dole and Gale M. Sinatra, "Reconceptualizing Change in Cognitive Construction of Knowledge"; and George J. Posner, Kenneth A. Strike, and William A. Gertzog, "Accommodation of a Scientific Conception."

least one thing in common: however wide the range of factors that have brought them about, they are all supported by some people's interpretations of the world, interpretations that cause them to act in ways that perpetuate the challenges we face. At the same time, not everyone sees the world the same way. People's minds can be changed. We must ask how the factors that shape these challenges come to have meaning, and then recognize that ultimately meaning is not static. It can be contested. Our goal is to engage in that process of contesting meaning, and this book is one way to achieve it. It is about shifting people's perspectives—our perspectives—so that the world we already know appears a bit *off*. That is, it is about shaking up the world we know so we can see what an outside viewer can see but we cannot. The tool to make this possible is cultural translation.

What is cultural translation? It is a term that means a lot of things to a lot of people.[2] To anthropologists, it is a way to explain a foreign culture to their readers. In the 1950s, for instance, British social anthropologists viewed the "problem of describing to others how members of a remote tribe think largely as one of translation, of making the coherence primitive thought has in the languages it really lives in, as clear as possible in our own."[3] By the 1980s, anthropologists had grown more reflexive, as books such as *Writing Culture* showed.[4] They began to address the Eurocentric biases in such observations, leading critics such as Edward Said to write that the "native point of view . . . is not an ethnographic fact only, is not a hermeneutical construct primarily or even principally; it is in large measure a continuing, protracted, and sustained adversarial resistance to the discipline and the praxis of anthropology."[5]

---

2 For overviews, see Sarah Maitland, *What Is Cultural Translation?* and Kyle Conway, "A Conceptual and Empirical Approach to Cultural Translation," and "Cultural Translation."

3 Godfrey Lienhardt, "Modes of Thought," 97.

4 James Clifford and George E. Marcus, eds., *Writing Culture: The Poetics and Politics of Ethnography.*

5 Edward Said, "Representing the Colonized: Anthropology's Interlocutors," 219–20.

Such critiques contributed to a different sense of the term, one more current in postcolonial studies, where it has come to describe a way to draw the logic of colonialism into question. Homi Bhabha, for instance, sees potential in the ways that immigrants introduce something new or foreign into the realm of the familiar as they live their "culture of the 'in-between', the minority position, [which] dramatizes the activity of culture's untranslatability."[6] In this way, for people like Bhabha, cultural translation holds the potential of challenging fixed notions of identity, especially in multicultural societies in Europe and North America.

To me, cultural translation means something more specific, and the definition I employ offers one possible synthesis of earlier notions by showing how taking others on their own terms can lead people to see their own identity in a new way. Cultural translation, as I describe it in this book, is a way to come to understand an object or text whose meaning derives from a shared interpretation of the world. It takes place through conversation and exchange.

Consider an illustration. Two people meet, and the first is interested in an object the second carries (figure 1). "What is that?" asks the first. "It's an X," says the second. "We use it when we do Y." "Neat," says the first, "that sounds like when we do Z." "Not exactly," answers the second, "it's more like this." Through such an exchange, the first person, substituting familiar references for the object in question, comes to understand (at least in an approximate way) how the second makes sense of it. In other words, cultural translation is a form of a give-and-take over meaning, or as I describe it elsewhere, in ways more in line with my scholarly argot, a semiotic economy where signs are exchanged for other signs on a basis negotiation rather than equivalence.[7] What makes it *translation* is the way we substitute one sign for another. What makes it *cultural* is the way the objects whose

6 Homi K. Bhabha, *The Location of Culture*, 224.

7 See Kyle Conway, "Cultural Translation, Global Television Studies, and the Circulation of Telenovelas in the United States."

meaning we are trying to discover are shared among members of different communities (although boundaries between communities might not be clearly marked). The type of cultural translation I am most interested in has clear ethical implications. It must, as Sarah Maitland insists, "have as its primary objective nothing short of the transformation of human hearts and minds."[8]

Figure 1. Cultural translation. Drawn by the author.

How do we reach this high bar? I propose that we engage in acts of wilful and strategic misreading. As I describe in the following sections, I'm writing to teachers and students. Our task is to return to the work of thinking, to reclaim our engagement with ideas. This task is complicated (and enriched) by the double status of cultural translation in this book: it is our primary object of study, but it also provides a mode of inquiry. That is, we can ask about the tools people use to arrive at a shared understanding of an object, and we can use those tools to understand the object of cultural translation itself. This reflexivity in turn opens up the question of what it means to

8 Maitland, *What Is Cultural Translation?* 53.

communicate. There is no more fundamental theoretical question than this, and in this respect, this book has a second area of focus, namely communication theory.

In the next sections, I talk about my audiences, and I untangle the relationship between the fields of translation studies and communication. Then I describe how teaching and research are two sides of the same coin and how they impose their own strategies to cultivate and refine the skills of purposeful reading. These strategies lead me finally to the idea of the parallax view, or the shift in perspective that makes wilful misreading possible. It is the parallax view that, ultimately, makes it possible to appreciate the art of communication in a polarized world.

Who Are We? What Is Our Role?

I want to be clear about something. When I say "we," it's not an abstraction. I mean real people leading real lives. What we're doing is theory, and we're doing it with the practical goal of changing people's minds by helping them shift perspective so that different facets of the world they know appear. In that respect, this is not a conventional book. It's an experiment. We will play—*I* will play—with tone and registers, and there will be lots of pictures. I argue (in chapter 1) that communication is always translation because we are always substituting one sign for another, and I want to substitute (among other things) pictures for words. I also argue that communication is rooted in the contingent moment. I am not an objective reporter. You (yes, *you*) are not a neutral observer. My first draft of this book was not a book at all. It was a series of lectures, complete with slides, that I delivered as part of a class (and will probably deliver again next semester). This is why, in this book, we are inextricably imbricated in indexicals, words that point to people or places or moments in time—"you," "I," "there," "here," "then," "now." Our relationship is real, even if temporally complicated. (My *right now* is not your *right now*. I am imagining you, future reader, imagining me, where my present is your past.) This guide is tactical only as long as we remember that relationship.

In other words, this book has a second purpose in addition to exploring cultural translation. It is a teaching tool, and it is addressed to a very specific audience: professors and students (specifically in cultural studies and translation studies). I am a professor. I have been teaching for a decade and a half. Right now I teach at the University of Ottawa. I was also once a student. I earned a bachelor's degree at the University of North Dakota (where, much later, I was also a professor), a master's at York University in Toronto, and a PhD at the University of Wisconsin. Why do I include these personal details? Because I am not talking to students or professors in an abstract sense. I am talking to my colleagues and friends, and I am talking to my students. I am concerned that, under pressure from politicians and corporations to turn university education into workforce training, we run the very real risk of abdicating our responsibility to train people to think or to do the work of thinking ourselves. Thus when I talk of students and professors, I don't want to make airy pronouncements about the university and society. I want to call for a return to the hard work of thinking. (If you're my student, remember—I am talking to *you*.) That's who we are. That's our role.

What is this work? Max Horkheimer and Theodor Adorno give us some sense of it in "The Culture Industry: Enlightenment as Mass Deception" when they talk about competing notions of artistic style. In a broad sense, they argue that the culture industry tells us what to think and how to feel. (By *culture industry* they mean the capitalists who sell us entertainment and shape how we understand the world.) Of course, we don't like to be told these things, and we flatter ourselves to believe that even if others can be duped, we cannot. But the culture industry is pernicious: it tricks us into thinking it's *our* idea to feel the way it wants us to feel. We trade real thinking for ersatz thinking. In the case of style, we trade an older concept for a newer, flatter one. In the past, *style* described the form an artist's statement took in the face of the world as its forces overwhelmed and negated her or him. It was individual and irreproducible. In contrast, *style* in contemporary culture describes the routinized elements that act like an artist's "brand." It is rule-bound and predictable. The culture industry banks on the fact that we consumers value consistency: we want to know what we're getting before we pay for it. In contrast, the work we teachers and students must do—the work I hope to encourage with this book—is to return to the type of engagement that produced the older form of artistic style.

You could raise objections, of course. If you're feeling ungenerous, you might say that professional academics like me are members of the worrying class. Our job is to generate alarm and then offer the very classes people should take to overcome their myopia. It's a cynical racket. We diagnose a problem people didn't even know they had and then sell them the tools to solve it.

But we needn't look to cynical scholars for this type of critique. A. O. Scott, film critic for the *New York Times*, wrote in a review of the Adam Sandler movie *Funny People*, in which Sandler's face is superimposed on a baby's body, that "there may be no more incisive rendering of Hollywood's self-image, and perhaps no truer, more damning mirror held up to the audience" than "that alarming man-baby, with the braying voice and the 5 o'clock shadow affixed to a pale, flabby, diaper-wrapped trunk." He goes on to say,

> Children are ceaselessly demanding, it's true; but they are also easily satisfied, and this combination of appetite and docility makes the child an ideal moviegoer. But since there are a finite number of literal children out there, with limited disposable income and short attention spans, Hollywood has to make or find new ones. And so the studios have, with increasing vigor and intensity, carried out a program of mass infantilization.[9]

9 A. O. Scott, "Open Wide: Spoon-Fed Cinema."

It's a powerful indictment.

There's a second objection to raise, one that comes from scholars themselves. If the field of cultural studies has taught us anything in the last three or four decades, it's that we should beware of these tales of gloom and doom. Audiences are active. We're *not* dupes. The media don't crack open our heads and dump in their content. Instead, we're active readers of different texts. We bring our experience to what we see and hear, and we interpret it through a lens that is partially of our own making, partially a function of our class, gender, race, and so on. We exercise our agency in constant tension with the world around us: even as our choices are constrained by the relations of power that link us to other people and groups, we still have choices to make. (Notably, this is the argument Stuart Hall makes in his essay "Encoding/Decoding," the subject of chapter 1.)

Still, people are susceptible to the persuasion of advertising, which tells us we'll be happy if only we buy the right deodorant or eat the right breakfast cereal. We are susceptible to fake news, or at the very least, to politicians who flatter us and tell us just how right we are. And, frankly, we don't like hearing from people who disagree with us.[10] In other words, our being duped isn't a given, but neither is our resistance. What matters is the way we exercise our agency, even when it is constrained. We have the capacity to develop strategies for active resistance, but it must be cultivated. Hence our role as professors and students. As Pierre Bourdieu writes, "intellectual discourse remains one of the most authentic forms of resistance to manipulation and a vital affirmation of the freedom of thought."[11] Hence this book.

10 See Jeremy A. Frimer, Linda J. Skitka, and Matt Motyl, "Liberals and Conservatives Are Similarly Motivated to Avoid Exposure to One Another's Opinions."

11 Pierre Bourdieu, *On Television*, 11.

Disciplining the Fields

I wrote above that I am addressing professors and students in cultural studies and translation studies. I hope others read this book, too, but if you know my audience, you'll have a better sense of the context for my argument.

So what constitutes these fields?

My formal training is in cultural studies as a subfield of communication, but my principal object of study has long been translation, and I publish often in translation studies journals. I have observed, as have others, that there is little exchange between these fields: "language and translation have been systematically neglected in the current literature on globalization."[12] Or "to a large extent, media, cultural and globalization studies have essentially ignored questions of language and translation."[13] Or again, "despite some early opportunities, translation and communication have had little to 'say' directly to one another."[14]

Even when cultural studies and translation scholars *do* examine the same things, they often talk past each other. Translation scholars, for instance, have catalogued the many ways translators are influenced by the ideologically charged sociocultural contexts within which they work, nuances that many cultural studies scholars fail to see. Translation scholars, on the other hand, often overlook the complex and contradictory forms of influence that texts have over audiences, forms that cultural studies scholars have deftly explored.

For that reason, I hope this book will be an opening point for a new line of inquiry, one that puts cultural studies and translation scholars into conversation. But it is important not to treat these two fields (or their objects of study) as existing a priori. They are contested, and they cohere by virtue of the disciplining habits of their

---

12 Esperança Bielsa and Susan Bassnett, *Translation in Global News*, 18.

13 Christof Demont-Heinrich, review of *Translation in Global News*, 402.

14 Ted Striphas, "Communication as Translation," 234.

members. That is, they are relatively closed systems: what makes people cultural studies scholars is that they attend cultural studies conferences and publish in cultural studies journals. What marks those conferences or journals as belonging to cultural studies is that cultural studies scholars go or publish there. Likewise for translation studies. These venues foster conversations among like-minded scholars who share specific preoccupations that motivate them to examine similar objects. Over time, these fields have developed differently in response to their respective preoccupations, and they bring different lenses to bear on their objects of study.[15]

Still, there is nothing inherent in either field that would prevent scholars from crossing over. Their closure is only relative, not absolute. There are certainly translation scholars such as Susan Bassnett whose work is shaped by cultural studies.[16] If we use departmental affiliation as an index of disciplinary affiliation, we also find a handful of cultural studies or communication scholars interested in translation.[17] But they are the exception that proves the rule: the paucity of exchange suggests that artificially maintained boundaries remain. If this book serves to encourage conversation, it will do so by revealing the points where each field's grindstones help sharpen the other field's tools.

---

15 On this development, see Stuart Hall, "Cultural Studies: Two Paradigms"; Kyle Conway, "Cultural Translation: Two Modes"; and Susan Bassnett, "The Translation Turn in Cultural Studies."

16 For example, Bielsa and Bassnett, *Translation in Global News*.

17 See, for example, Albert Moran, *New Flows in Global TV*; Ulrike Rohn, "Lacuna or Universal? Introducing a New Model for Understanding Cross-cultural Audience Demand"; Rainer Guldin, "From Transportation to Transformation: On the Use of the Metaphor of Translation Within Media and Communication Theory"; and Enrique Uribe-Jongbloed and Hernán David Espinosa-Medina, "A Clearer Picture: Towards a New Framework for the Study of Cultural Transduction in Audiovisual Market Trades."

Teaching and Research

This book grows out of the years I have spent teaching in these fields. I'm an unrepentant theorist. I make my students read texts they think are hard. I ask them to read closely and carefully, a practice they often find foreign, and I ask them to make claims and stake out a position, a practice they often find uncomfortable. In short, I ask them to argue with me and with the texts we read.

But that approach presumes they understand the texts in the first place, at least enough to have a toe-hold, something to ground their interpretations. This skill can be difficult, but it can be learned. It's complex and involves a range of tools, but the tools are simple enough. For instance, when I taught a master's-level survey of theory at the University of North Dakota, I gave students three steps to follow. As they read each text, I wanted them to look for three things, which I put in the syllabus itself:

- What questions does the author seek to answer?
- What arguments does the author make in answer to those questions?
- What critiques of the author's arguments can we offer?

On the first day of class, I explained that all the people we read had some question in mind they wanted to answer. Sometimes they stated their questions explicitly, but not always. If we could identify the questions, we could look for the answers they provided in the forms of the arguments they made.

Of the three tasks I gave them, the most difficult, I explained, was the third. *Critique*, in this case, means a wide range of things. Some possibilities include:

- Omission: what else might the author have included or discussed?
- External contradiction: how does the author's argument differ from our experience or from what we observe in the

world around us? How does it differ from other theorists' observations?

- Internal contradiction: does the logic of the author's argument contradict itself?

I wanted students to look for internal contradictions, but good writers hide them well. If students couldn't find them, external contradictions were valuable, too. In what way, I wanted to know, was their experience different from what the author argued? And if that was too hard—if they found the authors' account of their experience matched their own—they could always name something the authors left out. No one, I said, talks about radio. Or almost no one. So if they were stumped for a critique, they could always use that, as long as they were prepared to answer my inevitable follow-up question: what if the authors had talked about radio? What would they have said?

This approach turned theory into a form of τέχνη, or technē, the Greek word that gives us terms such as technique and technical, and that we might also gloss in this context as "learning-by-doing." Theory is a craft, like learning to play an instrument or learning to paint. Better yet, it's a process by which we cultivate and refine our understanding of the world by testing our explanations of the world against our experience.

I used this question-argument-critique approach for half a dozen years before seeing that there was something else—something deeper—going on. That approach taught students how to read strategically, but it didn't say what theory *was*. So now I begin my classes differently. I define *theory* by giving students three axioms:

1. Theory is an attempt to explain our experience of the world.
2. If the explanation theory offers doesn't match our experience, it's bad theory.
   (2a. In the end, it's all bad theory.)
3. We must refine our explanation to replace bad theory with better theory.

The first axiom is easy. We're doing theory when we try to explain the world. There are many ways to explain things. Communication theorists span the epistemological spectrum, from positivists anchored in an observable, knowable world to poststructuralists who question the basic assumptions that ground any claims we'd like to make.[18] (Epistemology is the branch of philosophy that asks how we know what we know. It is concerned with evidence and the validity of claims.) I tend toward the more skeptical end of the spectrum: we can know the world only through the mediation of our senses. For that reason, I draw on ideas of theory that come from the humanities, rather than the social sciences. In the social sciences, the scholar's task is to use the tools of method to discover something about the object of study. Research in the humanities—if it can be called "research" at all ("inquiry" or simply "scholarship" might be better)—inverts that task by asking the object of study to reveal something about the world. As John Durham Peters explains, "the point is less to illuminate" the texts we read "than to let them instruct us, by their distance and familiarity."[19] Consequently, as Jonathan Culler writes, theory in the humanities is interdisciplinary, analytical, and speculative (rather than falsifiable, as in the social sciences), and it provides a reflexive critique of common sense.[20]

In light of these differences, we can't evaluate humanistic theory as we do social scientific theory. Nowhere will we find p-values or statistical validity. Instead, we evaluate humanistic theory by testing our explanation, and when the explanation doesn't match our experience, the theory is bad. Hence the second axiom. But let's not be fooled.

---

18 Robert Craig, "Communication Theory as a Field"; and Diana Iulia Nastasia and Lana F. Rakow, "What Is Theory? Puzzles and Maps as Metaphors in Communication Theory."

19 John Durham Peters, *Speaking into the Air: A History of the Idea of Communication*, 36. Peters is concerned with Socrates and the Bible in the chapter I'm citing here, but given the approach he adopts throughout his book, I like to think that he wouldn't object to my expanding his point more broadly.

20 Jonathan Culler, *Literary Theory: A Very Short Introduction*, 14–15.

This axiom has a corollary: in the end, all theory is bad theory. That is, no explanation is complete. Theory always fails to explain something. Hence the third axiom: our job is to refine our explanations to replace bad theory with better theory. That improved explanation will also fail, of course, and we'll keep refining and refining and refining.[21] In this way, theory and experience mediate each other: theory explains the world we experience even as we test it against that experience. When I ask my students to argue with the authors we read (and with me!), that refinement is what I want them to do.

In simpler terms, the approach I try to teach marks a point where theory and practice intersect. To do theory is to understand (or explain) experience. We understand experience by practicing theory (in both senses of the word *practice*—"application of a trade" and "repetition of a skill"). And for me, the practice of theory takes on another dimension: it's teaching. It's leading students through these steps so they become second nature. It's also learning from students about the nature of theory as *technē*. I didn't start out with the question-argument-critique approach but instead developed it in response to the difficulties my students had when I assumed they understood texts as I did. I had forgotten what it's like to read difficult texts for the first time, and I developed the approach by thinking about how I myself had first encountered them. Similarly, I developed my three axioms in response to the way students worked through questions, arguments, and critiques.

As a result (as I write in the preface), this book is not a textbook, but it is pedagogical. It is about thinking and learning, activities in which we professors should be engaged as much as our students.

---

21 Of course, we can use social scientific approaches to critique and refine our explanations. Sometimes the challenge is finding ways to overcome the incommensurability of different scholarly paradigms—social scientists and humanists have different ways of approaching the world, not to mention different senses about what constitutes evidence or the types of claims it is useful to make. But this humanistic notion of theory, grounded in the conversation of critique and answers to critique, opens up ways to work through that impasse. For a sense of what this might look like from a more social scientific standpoint, see Craig, "Communication Theory as a Field."

The Parallax View

This book is about teaching and it's about how to change people's minds. It's a tactical guide whose two parts are linked by the challenge of opening people up to the possibility of seeing the world differently. Many of my students don't like theory (or *think* they don't) because they see no place for it in their lives. They come into my class filled with dread that I'll drone on and on about arcane knowledge that might as well be in a foreign language where they need to know just enough words to get by. My job is to help them recognize their unspoken assumptions about how the world works, in particular in relation to phenomena of communication. My job is also to help them see that their common sense understanding of communication is inadequate. They have been theorizing communication all along. It happens every time they explain some interaction where two people try to exchange information or when they try to persuade each other, to give two obvious examples. Inevitably, their explanations—their theories—miss something, and I want to provide tools to help them refine their understanding of what is going on.

In short, I want to help them observe something they might not have had any reason to observe before, namely their interpretive horizon, or those very assumptions that ground how they understand the world. ("Interpretive horizon" is a metaphor. Think of the horizon you see when you're outside. You probably don't pay much attention to it, but the things you do notice stand out because you see them against that horizon. It is in contrast to that horizon that they become visible. An interpretive horizon functions in the same way. You make assumptions about the world that are so basic you rarely think of them as such, but the things you do notice make sense because you see them against those assumptions or that horizon.) The task of cultural translation is the same: to prompt people to see what otherwise remains invisible, those basic conceptual building blocks that are so fundamental they fail to see them at all. Not that cultural translation is a type of education. To presume that it is, and to presume that I have some privileged view of the world, would be patronizing. Instead, cultural translation and teaching are examples of a broader phenomenon, that of our engagement with our own interpretive horizons.

I approach this task through the idea of a parallax view. The term comes from the Greek word παράλλαξις, meaning "variant." It refers to the way a set of objects looks different depending on the perspective of the viewer. Imagine you're walking down a street, and you spot a cool mural painted on the side of a building. Between you and the mural is a pole and a large silver shed. You continue to walk to get a better view. The shed, because it's closer to you, recedes quickly and no longer obstructs your view. The pole, which is farther from you than the shed but not as far as the mural, doesn't appear to move out of the way as quickly. So you keep walking, and eventually it too no longer obstructs your view. The mural, the farthest of these three objects from you, doesn't appear to move much at all, at least in relation to the shed and the pole. The three objects don't change position in relation to each other, but your perception of them does. That change in perspective is the parallax view (figure 2).

This approach is useful for understanding a wide range of phenomena because we can walk around other objects, too, so to speak. Consider the heroes in *Star Wars*.[22] We root for the ragtag team of rebels as they fight the darkly powerful Empire, which in its hubris has built the Death Star, a battle station designed to destroy entire planets. We identify with the rebels, as retired U.S. Air Force Lieutenant Colonel William Astore did in 1977, when the film was first released: "Like most young Americans then, I saw myself as a plucky rebel, a mixture of the free-wheeling, wisecracking Han Solo and the fresh-faced, idealistic Luke Skywalker."[23] But the truth is that almost everyone sees themselves in that role, even people on opposite sides

---

22 George Lucas, dir., *Star Wars* (1977)—later given the subtitle *A New Hope*.

23 William J. Astore, "Can You Spot the American Military in Your Favorite Sci-Fi Film? Hint: We're Always the Bad Guys."

Figure 2. Three pictures of a mural that provide an example of a parallax view. Photograph by the author. Courtesy of Amanda Osgood Jonientz.

of a conflict. Roy Scranton, a U.S. Army veteran who served in Iraq, writes of spending one Fourth of July "on the roof of a building in Baghdad that had once belonged to Saddam Hussein's secret police." He was thinking of *Star Wars*, and as he looked out over Baghdad, he came to see himself as he imagined Iraqis might see him: "I was the faceless storm trooper, and the scrappy rebels were the Iraqis."[24] Perspective is important.

Figure 3. Mural depicting Fatty Arbuckle, a silent movie star from the 1910s that also provides an example of parallax view, 2014. Photograph by the author. Artist Joel Jonientz.

This approach also helps us see why other approaches would fall short. Isn't it presumptuous, you might object, to think we can— or should—change someone else's mind? Wouldn't it be better to explore how others think so we can find some common ground for negotiating meaning? Perhaps. But people can understand others' perspectives and still disagree. More important, even to reach the

24 Roy Scranton, "'Star Wars' and the Fantasy of American Violence."

point where they can find common ground, they must first see the world from a different perspective, to understand how their opponents—like them!—see themselves as the rebels in *Star Wars*, too. Cultural translation remains a valuable tool to change people's minds. (We will revisit this point in the book's concluding chapter.)

Strategies of Misreading

So how do we walk around *ideas* to see them anew? How do we come to see our world so it appears a little strange? We start by recognizing something fundamental about the texts we read.[25] We cannot know an author's mind. We cannot know an author's intention. Although the words the author has written might seem to represent her or his intention, they are open to interpretation. Words mean too many things. Or as Paul Ricoeur explains,

> When I speak, I realize only a part of the potential signified; the rest is erased by the total signification of the sentence, which operates as the unit of speaking. But the rest of the semantic possibilities are not canceled; they float around the words as possibilities not completely eliminated.[26]

If this is the case, then what *can* we know? We can know the words we have in front of us, words that are assembled into a concrete, stable form. And we can know what others have said about them (although, there, too, we can know only *what* they've said, not their intentions). In order to walk around the text—better yet, to walk around the ideas within the text—it is enough to offer an interpretation that is at once consistent with it but different from how others have responded. That is, our strategy should be to misread a text by reading against

25 My analysis in this section is indebted to Sarah Maitland's *What Is Cultural Translation?*

26 Paul Ricoeur, "The Problem of Double Meaning as Hermeneutic Problem and as Semantic Problem," 71.

the interpretations that people have had before. We must misread strategically, so that misreading becomes a more sophisticated type of cultural translation. It is a more strategic type of exchange than in my illustration above, one that has value when one of the people in the exchange is resistant to the idea that things might be other than she or he imagines them.

That is the exercise I undertake in the rest of this book. In chapter 1, I misread Stuart Hall's "Encoding/Decoding." Hall was concerned with a common sense way of thinking about television, one related to the classic sender-message-receiver model of communication. He read against this model in ways that influenced the entire field of media and cultural studies, where scholars have spent a lot of time looking at how viewers decode television. I read against those scholars to arrive at a new interpretation of "Encoding/Decoding," namely that every time we speak or write, we are in fact translating. We are substituting one use of a word (ours) for another (that of the person we're talking to). This misreading serves two purposes: it simultaneously illustrates and authorizes the strategy I advocate.

Thus the first chapter focuses on communication theory in order to show how misreading can be a conceptual tool. The second chapter looks for theory in an unexpected place: George Orwell's treatise on language, appended to his novel *Nineteen Eighty-Four*. If my misreading of Hall suggests ways cultural translation can open new horizons, my misreading of Orwell's book—not as a novel with a treatise on language appended but as a translation manual with a novel appended—shows how it can also close them off.

The chapters that follow are about how people have used these tools to induce a parallax view in others. Chapter 3 describes how they have used art to do so in constructive ways. It focuses on a Russian artist who shocks his audiences by subjecting himself to great pain in very public performances, giving them a new perspective to ground their view of the world (and changing the mind even of one of the cops sent to interrogate him). His tactic is conceptually simple:

he asks viewers to reconsider their ideas about his actions, some of which break the law, in light of a different higher-order principle—to see them in the context of ethics rather than crime and punishment. Chapter 4 describes the opposite: it is about perspective unmoored. It is about the odd path taken by the phrase *fake news* after the 2016 U.S. election. In the days following the vote, the phrase described stories that were made up. People wanted to encourage others to pay attention *real* news—to things that actually happened. But the new president of the United States quickly took the phrase and used it to evoke something different. He used it whenever he disagreed with a story, creating a space of extreme relativism, where the criteria people used to evaluate claims about the world had less to do with evidence and more to do with whether they agreed politically with the people making the claims.

Finally, the last chapter returns to where the book began. It offers a metatheoretical account of the performative dimensions of my argument (that is, it relates the *form* of my argument back to the question, *what is theory?*). It proposes an epistemology of jumping in: if theory is a foreign language, the best way to learn it is through immersion. Even if we don't have all the tools we need, necessity helps us discover them as we go. (Not coincidentally, cultural translation is also best understood from this standpoint.) It's for that reason that throughout the book, I try to provoke as much as to explain. I give examples to encourage an inductive form of reasoning so students will do the work of connecting ideas themselves. Thus in the conclusion I look at the ways this book develops an explanation of communication and at applications of the tools it identifies. I want to help students see how theory encourages a parallax view of the world, not to mention communication. The final chapter connects the dots, from beginning to end, and then turns students loose.

Communication Is Translation
(So Please Mind the Gap)

What you are reading is a translation. It began as a lesson in one of my classes, replete with slides, and now I have turned it into a book chapter.

No, that's not right. It began much earlier. My lesson reworked a keynote talk I gave at a conference, and my keynote reworked an opaque theoretical article I published in the *International Journal of Communication.*[1] And that article reworked Stuart Hall's encoding/decoding model to see what it had to reveal about translation. (For that matter, so does this chapter.) And Hall's model reworked Marx's take on political economy in the *Grundrisse*. (And the *Grundrisse* reworked older versions of political economy, which reworked . . . which reworked . . . which reworked . . .)

In other words, there is no single point of origin. What you are reading is the result of one long series of transformations and substitutions: encoding/decoding substitutes for the *Grundrisse*; my

---

1 Kyle Conway, "Encoding/Decoding as Translation." But even this genealogy is not quite right. There is an intermediate step: an earlier version of this chapter appeared as "Communication Is Translation, or, How to Mind the Gap" in *Palabra Clave* 20, no. 3 (2017): 622–44. It is reproduced here with the kind permission of the journal.

article substitutes for encoding/decoding; my keynote substitutes for my article; my lesson substitutes for my keynote; and now, this chapter substitutes for my lesson. It is a translation. It could not be otherwise.

It is no coincidence I'm describing it as a translation. My purpose here is to demonstrate the strategy of the parallax view by asking what would happen if cultural studies scholars talked about translation. Or, more to the point, what would a theory of translation look like if it were grounded in the field of cultural studies? The answer I give is as performative as it is expository. That is, the logic that shapes my answer also applies to this chapter itself, in that it shapes its form. Like every other form of discourse, this chapter participates in an economy of substitution—of trading words, sentences, and ideas for other words, sentences, and ideas. When I speak of translation, that trading is what I mean, and in that respect, my opening examples are strategic: they show how translation works before I even say what I think it is. The examples I choose in the sections that follow are also strategic: they illustrate a key relationship between signs by moving between semiotic systems (for example, between words and pictures or between formal and informal linguistic registers).

So what, then, is that relationship? What exactly is translation? To answer that question, I propose three axioms:

1. To use a sign is to transform it.
2. To transform a sign is to translate it.
3. Communication is translation.

In the following sections, I approach these axioms by providing two parallax views. I begin by describing an early model of communication—the sender-message-receiver model—developed by electrical engineers in the 1940s as a way to improve the telephone networks they were building. Then, to work through these axioms, I peer at the sender-message-receiver model from a different angle, the one provided by Stuart Hall's "Encoding/Decoding."[2] It serves as the basis for a materialist approach to semiotics, which in turn provides the conceptual tools to take a new look at "Encoding/Decoding" itself. The point is to pry open the act of speaking and responding to see how signs are transformed when we use them. Taking my cues from Hall, whose essay has had a profound impact on scholarly notions of politics, I finish by arguing that the transformation and substitution of signs opens up a space for a politics of invention, where we can rethink our relation to cultural others so that people we once feared can find their place in the communities we claim as our own.

Sender-Message-Receiver

One of the most influential models of communication developed from efforts by electrical engineers in the 1940s to find ways to make telephones work better. They were asking a technical question, namely how to overcome the noise that interfered with the transmission of information, especially as telephone lines got longer and noise increased. They wanted to calculate the point where signals were transmitted with maximum efficiency, but they had to balance efficiency with redundancy. The most efficient transmission would be one where each element of a message is sent once, but only once. The problem is that the channels used for transmission introduce extraneous signals. If each element is sent only once, the receiver has no way to know whether it has been corrupted because there is no way to confirm that the message received is right. (The receiver would have to ask "Did you say . . . ?" and then repeat the message, thus sending it more than once.) Think of the children's game of telephone, where one person whispers a message to a second, who

2 See Stuart Hall, "Encoding and Decoding in the Television Discourse," and "Encoding/Decoding."

whispers it to a third, who whispers it to a fourth, and so on.[3] It's an efficient system (each person whispers the message once), but the message the last person receives is always garbled. And since there is no feedback from one person to the next, the last person cannot know for sure whether (or where) it is garbled until the first person tells everyone what she or he said.

One solution to this problem is to build in forms of redundancy, especially in the form of feedback, although doing so makes the transmission less efficient. Imagine again our game of telephone. If the second person repeated the message back to the first, making sure to get it exactly right, and then the third person repeated it back to the second, and the fourth to the third, and so on, the message would likely be less garbled when it arrived, but it would take much longer for it to work its way down the line.

To solve the problems they faced in the 1940s, engineers proposed the sender-message-receiver model. Claude Shannon published the first iteration in 1948, which Warren Weaver helped popularize in the years that followed. A transmitter, they said, transforms information into a message that can be sent through a channel like a copper wire. The receiver then transforms the message back into its original form. Or, to use Weaver's terms, "The function of the transmitter is to encode, and that of the receiver to decode, the message" (figure 4).[4] But just as in the example above, no transmission is exact. There is always noise, and it takes feedback from the receiver to the transmitter to be confident the information is transmitted correctly, or at least that any corruption is kept to a minimum, as Shannon showed with a set of mathematical formulas for determining the optimal levels of efficiency and redundancy.

Although this model has been influential in communication theory, it has drawbacks. The most important, from a cultural studies

3 My Canadian students call this game "broken telephone." That name seems better suited to the way messages break down.

4 Warren Weaver, "The Mathematics of Communication," 13.

point of view, is that the "semantic aspects of communication are irrelevant to the engineering problem."[5] In other words, Shannon was concerned only with the reliable transmission of information, which for him could be any set of symbols, whether they were imbued with meaning or not. He was not concerned with content, which could be "fsd jklrwiouv kldf sa" (a string of letters I produced by smashing my fingers on the keyboard) just as well as "To sleep, perchance to dream." In either case, the engineering problem remained the same. (Weaver, to be fair, did address the possibility of meaning in his efforts to popularize Shannon's model. "The formal diagram of a communication system," he wrote, "can, in all likelihood, be extended to include the central issues of meaning and effectiveness.")[6]

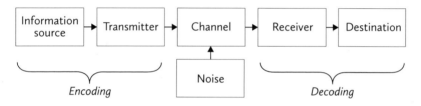

Figure 4. Sender-message-receiver model developed by Shannon and Weaver showing the steps of message transmission. Adapted from Weaver (1949, p. 12–13).

The question of meaning would be Stuart Hall's point of departure, the pivot around which he would walk to see the sender-message-receiver model from a new perspective.

Theoretical Foundations: A Materialist Approach to Semiotics

The axioms I propose above have two starting points: materialism (a philosophical stance that grounds analysis in people's lived

5 C. E. Shannon, "A Mathematical Theory of Communication," 379.

6 Weaver, "Mathematics of Communication," 14.

experience) and semiotics (the study of how meaning functions).[7] The materialism comes, as mentioned in the introduction, from Stuart Hall's reaction to the sender-message-receiver model in his essay "Encoding and Decoding in the Television Discourse," better known in its revised form, "Encoding/Decoding." Hall argues that television programs are only one moment in a circuit that links producers and viewers in a specific social context. The meaning with which they imbue a program is grounded in this context.

The encoding/decoding model, in fact, is an application of Marx's political economy, as laid out in his introduction to the *Grundrisse*.[8] Marx's insight was that production and consumption were not independent moments in the circulation of commodities but were, on the contrary, mutually constitutive—one could not exist without the other. On the one hand, to give an example, the objects a cobbler produces become a pair of shoes in a meaningful sense only when someone puts them on her or his feet. In this way, the act of consumption is implicated in the act of production. On the other, the cobbler produces shoes in such a way as to influence how people wear them, by altering materials and styles to create a demand. In this way, production is implicated in the act of consumption.

Hall extends this analysis to television. He describes the moments of production and consumption—"encoding" and "decoding"—as mutually constitutive. (Note the common language with Shannon and Weaver.) Producers encode certain meanings into shows, but viewers do not necessary decode them as intended. Nonetheless, the moments of production and consumption are linked in that producers anticipate viewers' reactions, and viewers interpret shows in

---

7 Note how this use of the term *materialism* (which derives from Marx's work) differs from our everyday sense of materialism as an undue focus on material goods at the expense of relationships with people that fulfill us on a deeper level. This is one point where I must ask my students—my first readers—to remember that I am using the word differently. Otherwise, this discussion is likely to be confusing.

8 Karl Marx, "Introduction," in *Grundrisse: Foundations of the Critique of Political Economy*, esp. sec. (2).

part based on their knowledge of producers. The shows themselves are complex signs that link producers and viewers, who also operate within a shared social context.

In short, production and consumption are linked in a relationship of mutual dependence. Hall frames these forms of mutual influence as a circuit, which he illustrates in figure 5.

Note that I have adapted the figure Hall presents in the earlier version of his essay (from 1973), which differs from its better known counterpart (in "Encoding/Decoding" from 1980) in one important way: it has an arrow that runs from the factors that influence decoding to those that influence encoding. In other words, it completes the circuit by making the influence of decoding on encoding explicit.

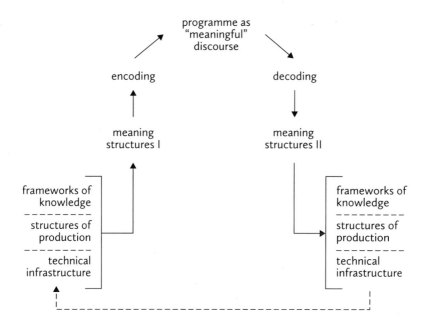

Figure 5. Encoding/decoding model by Hall showing the circuit of meaning generated in a television program. Illustration by Stuart Hall, "Encoding and Decoding in the Television Discourse," *CCCS Stencilled Occasional Papers* 7 (1973, p.4).

Also note the way Hall's diagram looks like the sender-message-receiver model, but all stretched out and twisted. Shannon and Weaver were concerned with how a channel transmitted information. Hall is concerned with how a program becomes a channel, or better yet a medium, for transmitting meaning. But he also draws the idea of transmission into question. Shannon and Weaver were concerned with the steps a transmitter took to encode information and the steps the receiver took to decode it. Hall breaks the moments of transmission and reception down by looking at the factors that shape them, relative to people's frameworks of knowledge, the structures of production in which they are embedded, and the technical infrastructure available to them. By peering at the sender-message-receiver model from a different angle, one where meaning predominates, he helps us see that Shannon and Weaver's primary question—how can we transmit information with the least distortion?—is not the right question at all, at least not if we are concerned with meanings that are contested.

Hall's attention to the factors that influence encoding and decoding, which all relate to the material conditions of textual production and meaning-making, is what makes his model materialist. Nevertheless, the psychological aspects of meaning—how programs evoke ideas for viewers—remain unclear. Hence my second starting point, the idea of a sign. Here I draw on American philosopher Charles Peirce, who says,

> A sign . . . is something which stands to somebody for something in some respect or capacity. It addresses somebody, that is, creates in the mind of that person an equivalent sign, or perhaps a more developed sign. That sign which it creates I call the *interpretant* of the first sign.[9]

Consider my stick-figure heroes in figure 6. The star spoken by Hero 1 (on the left) is the sign because it evokes something for Hero 2 (on the right). And the ideas it evokes for Hero 2 are also signs, as they

9 Charles Peirce, *The Philosophy of Peirce: Selected Writings*, 99.

evoke still more ideas, which evoke more, and more, and more. (My image cannot capture the full chain of associations.) This is what Peirce means when he speaks of the interpretant.[10]

Figure 6. A sign used by Hero 1 evokes a series of interpretants for Hero 2. Drawn by the author.

It is useful to make a distinction here between the material and subjective aspects of the sign. On the one hand, there is the material side—the specific patterns of vibrating sound that hit our eardrums in the case of a word, for instance, or the patterns of light and sound in the case of a television program, or Hero 1's star.[11] On the other, there is the subjective side—what a speaker or producer hopes to evoke by using a given material sign (a word, a TV program, etc.), and what that material sign evokes for a listener or viewer, as in the case of Hero 2's chain of associations. The subjective aspect of the sign consists in the string of interpretants evoked by the material sign.[12]

---

10 If my heroes bring to mind Randall Munroe's brilliant webcomic *xkcd* (https://xkcd.com), then they are signs and *xkcd* is their interpretant.

11 Peirce would call this material sign the *representamen*. For an overview of Peirce's terminology, see Floyd Merrell, "Charles Sanders Peirce's Concept of the Sign," 29–39.

12 This distinction between "material" and "subjective" signs needs clarification. First, it looks like Ferdinand de Saussure's distinction (in *Course in General*

Axiom 1: To Use a Sign Is to Transform It

How does a materialist approach drawn from Marx's political economy and from 1970s-era reactions to a 1940s-era engineering problem relate to the idea of a sign made up of material and subjective parts? As Hall demonstrates, the televisual sign links producers and viewers. Its meaning is a point of negotiation between them, which is shaped by their knowledge and expectations of each other. But this negotiation over meaning is not unique to television. V. N. Vološinov, in *Marxism and the Philosophy of Language*, argues that we negotiate the meaning of every sign. He gives the example of a word:

> A word presents itself not as an item of vocabulary but as a word that has been used in a wide variety of utterances by co-speaker A, co-speaker B, co-speaker C and so on, and has been variously used in the speaker's own utterances.[13]

So when Hero 1 on the left uses a sign (figure 7), Hero 2 on the right responds by taking into account how Hero 1 used it (figure 8). If Hero 2 uses it again, it is with the earlier exchange in mind, at least partially.

But we are more than just reactive: when we talk to people, we are also predictive. As Mikhail Bakhtin points out:

> When constructing my utterance, I try actively to determine this response [that is, the response of the person I am talking to]. Moreover, I try to act in accordance with the response I

Linguistics) between signifier and signified, but it is not. Strictly speaking, Saussure's signifiers are "sound images," whereas material signs exist in the world outside speakers' psyches. Similarly, Saussure's signifieds are concepts evoked by sound images, but they do not operate in a chain, as in Peirce's conception. Second, I have chosen not to call material signs "objective" (as the inverse of "subjective") because the term would be misleading to the degree it implied that the meanings of materials signs were fixed. Finally, this distinction is only heuristic. V. N. Vološinov (in *Marxism and the Philosophy of Language*) demonstrates that material conditions always impinge on our subjective experience of language, so much so that language is a material fact that exists outside of speakers' individual psyches.

13 Vološinov, *Marxism and the Philosophy of Language*, 70.

anticipate, so this anticipated response, in turn, exerts an active influence on my utterance (I parry objections that I foresee, I make all kinds of provisos, and so forth).[14]

Figure 7. Hero 1 asks Hero 2 a question. Drawn by the author.

Figure 8. Hero 2 answers the question posed by Hero 1, using Hero 1's word in a subtly changed context. Drawn by the author.

In other words, just as TV producers (according to Hall) shape their programs in partial anticipation of what viewers will think, we shape our utterances (whatever form they might take) in partial

14 Mikhail Bakhtin, *Speech Genres and Other Late Essays*, 95.

anticipation of how others will react. (And we do so in a given social context, to return to Hall's model.)

Thus our heroes continue to pass a word back and forth, each time reacting to what the other has said and taking that reaction into account. Perhaps they have a discussion. Perhaps Hero 2 is really a jerk, or maybe just clumsy with Hero 1's feelings. Maybe Hero 2 is not really a hero at all (figure 9). So Hero 1 leaves, while Hero 2 calls after Hero 1 in vain (figure 10).

Figure 9. Hero 1 responds to Hero 2, repeating the same word in a still-evolving context, and concludes that Hero 2 is a jerk. Drawn by the author.

And, finally, Hero 2 is left to replay the scene, to figure out what went wrong. The sign means something for Hero 2 that it did not mean before. At the beginning of the conversation, it did not evoke regret or puzzlement, and now it does (figure 11). This is what I mean when I say "to use a sign is to transform it." The material aspect of a sign may remain the same over the course of an exchange, but the subjective aspect does not. And if the material aspect is one side of a sign, and the subjective aspect the other, then the pair has changed.

The sign—the pair together, as a unit—is different from what it was before.[15]

Hero 1   Hero 2

Figure 10. Hero 1 has had enough and walks away. Hero 2 objects to Hero 1's conclusion about their exchange. Drawn by the author.

Hero 2

Figure 11. Now alone, Hero 2 considers the exchange with Hero 1 and wonders what went wrong. Drawn by the author.

---

15 My formulation here seems to suggest a constantly expanding interpretant, but that's not necessarily the case. People stop using signs in certain circumstances, too. Meanings can contract, as chapter 4 shows in the case of the phrase *fake news* before and immediately following the 2016 U.S. election.

Axiom 2: To Transform a Sign Is to Translate It

And so we arrive at my second axiom: to transform a sign is to translate it.

Perhaps this axiom appears counterintuitive or based on a notion of translation that I have had to wrangle and contort. In fact, the opposite is true. What do I mean by *translation*? Exactly what it means in a conventional sense—the substitution of one sign (or one set of signs) for another. We transform signs by using them: their subjective dimension changes because Hero 2 has to take into account the use by Hero 1, something Hero 1 did not have to do. Thus the transformed sign substitutes for the sign that came before. The change might be small (in fact, most of the time it is), but we can also imagine more dramatic cases, such as when Hero 1 tells Hero 2 something life-changing, and Hero 2 must make sense of a new configuration of their symbolic universe. (By "symbolic universe" I mean the ordered set of beliefs people have that shape how they make sense of objects and events.) Think of Luke Skywalker in *The Empire Strikes Back*.[16] The sign *father* changes dramatically when he learns who Darth Vader really is.

Or think of how the sign *translation* has changed for you since the beginning of this chapter. As you think of questions you want to ask and points you want me to clarify, you are taking into account what I have said. The chain of associations—that is, the interpretants—the sign *translation* evokes for you has grown. Perhaps not dramatically, but it is larger nonetheless. The subjective aspect of the sign has changed, which means the material/subjective pair as a unit has changed. I have substituted a new use of the term for an older use. At the risk of being too clever, I would say I have translated *translation*.

16 Irvin Kershner, dir., *The Empire Strikes Back* (1980).

Axiom 3: Communication Is Translation

Here we arrive at my third axiom: "Communication is translation."
In all truth, the first two axioms form a syllogism, from which the
third derives. If we use a sign, we transform it. If we transform a sign,
we translate it. Therefore, if we use a sign—that is, if we communicate—we translate it. In other words (what a revealing phrase—"in
other words"), communication is translation.

In some ways, this assertion is not new. George Steiner, in his
influential book *After Babel*, argues,

> Any model of communication is at the same time a model of
> translation, of a vertical or horizontal transfer of significance.
> No two historical epochs, no two social classes, no two localities
> use words and syntax to signify the same things, to send iden-
> tical signals of valuation and inference. Neither do two human
> beings.[17]

Paul Ricoeur, in *On Translation*, goes further. Because the sign I use
never evokes the exact same thing for you as for me, we constantly
misunderstand each other. We say what we have to say, but then we
also have to explain what we mean. Sometimes we have to explain
our explanation, until we are as satisfied as we can be that we have
gotten our message through:

> It is always possible *to say the same thing in another way*. . . . That
> is why we have never ceased making ourselves clear, making our-
> selves clear with words and sentences, making ourselves clear to
> others who do not see things from the same angle as we do.[18]

Language is reflexive, and *tant mieux*—if we could not talk about
what we mean, especially when we see that our point has not gotten
through, communication would grind to a halt.

---

17 George Steiner, *After Babel: Aspects of Language and Translation*, 47.
18 Paul Ricoeur, *On Translation*, 25–27.

Note, however, that Steiner and Ricoeur make an assumption that I do not. They presume there is an active agent, someone thinking about the meaning of signs, in that they are explaining, "When I said X, what I really meant was . . . " In effect, they are translating X by "say[ing] the same thing in another way." But if each use of a sign transforms it, then there is no need for an active agent. Transformation and translation take place whether we think about what signs mean or not. Hero 1 says "*" and Hero 2 adds that use to their series of interpretants, so when Hero 2 says "*" it is not an identical sign (figure 12).

Figure 12. The meaning of a word evolves as two people converse, illustrating how translation takes the form of transformative substitution. Drawn by the author.

A Politics of Invention

Why dwell on this seemingly minor point? As Stuart Hall showed with television, the gap between the producer's intended meaning and the meaning a show evokes for a viewer is the condition of possibility for acts of resistance. Because we are intelligent human beings, and because we have our own experience which differs from that of the people who produce television, we do not have to agree with what we see on TV. In fact, we can take what we see and arrive at radically different—and equally plausible—interpretations as we reconfigure meanings to match with our experience and meet our expectations.

That idea of resistance leads me to a further observation: the gap between signs is productive, something we can put to use. We must (as the London Underground reminds us) mind the gap. How do we do that? That question is the point of this book, which approaches it as an empirical question: how have people put that gap to use? How have they used it to persuade others to see the world differently? These questions get to the heart of what rhetoricians, drawing on Aristotle, describe as *invention* (or *inventio* in Latin), by which they mean the generation of arguments.[19] It is one of five steps in the process of crafting a persuasive speech, the other four of which include arranging arguments (*dispositio* in Latin), matching them stylistically to the audience (*elocutio*), remembering them (*memoria*), and finally delivering them effectively (*pronuntiatio*). (We will explore Aristotle's notion of invention in more depth in chapter 3.)

Aristotle says that rhetoric is the art of persuasion, or "the faculty of observing in any given case the available means of persuasion," and rhetorical invention is the ability to find the right words in a particular context.[20] In this sense, persuasion is contingent on circumstances, which change from one situation to the next. It is grounded in the moment of speaking and therefore not knowable in advance. It is a matter of mastering different tools that help you think on your toes.

My contention is that the gap between a speaker's sign and a listener's sign is a space where we can practice a specific type of invention.

19 We tend not to use *invention* this way in everyday speech. I anticipate that one challenge for my students will be to accept that the term means something other than what they expect. My use of this older sense risks falling into the trap I describe in the first paragraph of the introductory chapter, namely, that it will have no place within their pre-existing symbolic universe. That is, if they read it as invention in a contemporary sense—say, some scientific innovation for which one might receive a patent—the argument I'm presenting will be confusing. They will need to set aside what they know to see the term from a new angle.

20 Aristotle, *Rhetoric*, book I, part 2.

Cultural translation, as a number of people have observed, has a certain utopian potential.[21] For instance, it opens up the possibility for acts of hospitality by allowing us to speak against the hegemonic norms of identity that prevent people who appear different or foreign from joining "our" group, whichever it is. It is a matter of identifying the "available means of persuasion." This act is fundamentally creative, and it has important ethical implications.

Let me illustrate with an example, which comes from Bertolt Brecht, by way of translation studies scholars Boris Buden and Stefan Nowotny.[22] In his poem "The Democratic Judge," Brecht describes an Italian immigrant to the United States who is applying for citizenship, although he does not speak English. The man stands before the judge, and the judge asks him questions about the United States as part of a citizenship test. "What is the eighth amendment?" the judge asks. "1492," he answers because he does not understand.

The setting of the exchange is symbolically important. The applicant is asking for admission into a new national community. It is the culmination of a long process of asking—from immigration, to integration (in different senses, as he does not speak English), to finally making a formal request. Thus when he is refused, according to Buden and Nowotny, it is a literal refusal of his symbolic request, one more refusal on top of all the others he has faced since arriving in his new home.

So the man returns later, and the judge asks another question. "Who was the winning general of the Civil War?"

Again the man answers, "1492." Again, he is refused.

He returns a third time, and the scene repeats itself. "How long do presidents serve?" "1492."

But something happens for the judge. It is a moment of invention. When the man returns a fourth time, according to Brecht:

---

21 Most notably, Homi Bhabha makes this argument in *The Location of Culture*.

22 Boris Buden and Stefan Nowotny, "Cultural Translation: An Introduction to the Problem."

The judge, who liked the man, realised that he could not
Learn the new language, asked him
How he earned his living and was told: by hard work. And so
At his fourth appearance the judge gave him the question:
When
Was America discovered? And on the strength of his correctly
answering
1492, he was granted his citizenship.[23]

The judge looks at the situation and assesses it. He looks at the tools available to him. He is a judge, so he cannot break the law, but he takes pity on the man and decides the United States would be better for having him as a citizen. Given those constraints, he contrives a question—one that is in line with all those he has already asked, although today it would be a bit anachronistic—that the man can answer. The judge has worked within the constraints imposed on him to make a stranger no longer strange, a new member of the national community.

Buden and Nowotny say that the judge has found "a correct question" for "a wrong answer."[24] The judge has taken advantage of the gap between one use of the sign *1492* and the next. Over the course of his interactions with the man, the sign *1492* has come to have a richer set of interpretants. In each case, but especially in the question that sets up the final, "correct" use, he has taken his previous interactions with the man into account. Hence the expanded set of associations (figure 13). What is important is that the judge finds a way to make the evolution of the sign's meaning productive—it becomes a tool in an act of inclusion. It is not hard to think of other situations where such invention has value, or where scholars can use this idea to gain insight into our interactions with groups who are marked as "different" or "foreign."

23 Brecht, quoted in Buden and Nowotny, "Cultural Translation," 206–7.
24 Ibid., 207.

Figure 13. Bertolt Brecht's judge devises the correct question for a wrong answer. Illustration of judge adapted from Ward (1899, "Men of the Day No. 756: Caricature of Mr. Franklin Lushington [1823–1901]"). Source: Wikimedia Commons.

Conclusion: The Logic of Substitution-Transformation

In this chapter's introduction, I wrote that this chapter is a translation, a reworking of a lesson, which reworked an article, which reworked ... which reworked ... which reworked. ... Why have I made the same argument more than once? What is the value of the repetition? What does this version offer that older versions (or past links in the chain) did not?

One answer to these questions is relatively superficial. My earlier elaboration relied on a deductive mode of reasoning.[25] It was a series of literal and implied "if-then" statements. I crafted the version you have just read to rely more on induction—I proceed by examples and build to my conclusions from there. I hope this version achieves a different effect—I hope it left blanks that you filled in. In short, I hope it demonstrated invention as much as explained it.

Another answer goes still further. In this chapter's introduction I also wrote, *What would a theory of translation look like if it were grounded in the field of cultural studies? The answer I give is as performative as it is expository. That is, the logic that shapes my answer also applies to this chapter itself, in that it shapes its form.* How does this logic apply? This question and these statements are signs, by Peirce's definition, in that they "stand to somebody for something in some respect or capacity." Their use here differs from their use in my introduction, if I have succeeded in my translation, because they evoke something new for you. The first time, I had hinted at but not laid out the logic of transformation-substitution. You had to take my assertion on faith. Now, I hope, it stands on its own merits.

This logic is what authorizes the theoretical moves I make in the following chapters. The parallax views I produce or describe depend on the multiplicity of meanings of any given sign, which comes about because of the transformation signs undergo with each use. We can gaze at meaning from another angle because signs always mean more

---

25 Conway, "Encoding/Decoding as Translation."

than what the people who use them intend, a semiotic excess that provides an excess of perspectives, if we choose to explore them.

In sum, the questions of invention that follow from this conception of translation are ones I think we should be asking in the fields of communication and cultural studies. If we develop a theory of translation that responds to our concerns, and if we bring the tools we have developed to bear on such a theory, we can conceive new approaches to politics and ethics. In a world where the forces of globalization are constantly accelerating, and where we come into greater and greater contact with people unlike ourselves, few tasks could be as important as this one.

But nothing guarantees our success, and as I write in the next chapter, the same logic of transformation substitution can close off the very potential that invention seems to open up.

Newspeak as a Manual
for Translation

The last chapter ends on a hopeful note: cultural translation is the tool we use to shift people's perspectives so they see the world differently. It's a technique for opening a space where we can welcome people who aren't like us, whom we've excluded in the past.

But there's a risk in that perception. It leaves open the question of who "we" are. I'm presuming my readers are like me in that they want to overcome the divisions we impose upon the world when we separate people into categories like *us* and *them*. That assumption is false. If recent politics has shown anything, it's that people are worried about outsiders causing them to lose their identity. They want to maintain those categories. The Rassemblement national in France (formerly the Front national), the Freiheitliche Partei Österreichs in Austria, Alternative für Deutschland in Germany, and the UK Independence Party in Great Britain have all made electoral gains by appealing to nativist sentiments and exploiting people's fears of outsiders.[1]

There's a second risk to consider. The processes of transformation described in the last chapter work in more than one direction.

1 See Kyle Conway, "Modern Hospitality."

Cultural translation—the replacement of one sign by another—can close down the potential for exchange, too. It can make oppression possible. It can exclude.

This chapter is about that second direction. It's about George Orwell's novel *Nineteen Eighty-Four*, which tells the story of a man's struggle in a dystopian future where free thought is no longer possible, having been undermined by linguistic engineering, probing surveillance, and unrelenting violence. This chapter focuses on the appendix "The Principles of Newspeak," which describes the purpose of the novel's invented language as making "heretical thought"—that is, any thought not consistent with the ideology of the totalitarian government—"literally unthinkable, at least so far as thought is dependent on words" (*Nineteen Eighty-Four*, 198).[2] In that respect, it shifts our perspective on *Nineteen Eighty-Four* by treating it as a translation manual with a novel appended. "The Principles of Newspeak" is about how to replace words strategically to reduce the range of things people can think, which is to say, to *translate* them. The novel illustrates the ends to which such translation can be put, especially when its practitioners also have the means to surveil and torture those who think beyond the parameters set by the authorities. It serves as a warning about the logic of cultural translation, whose utopian potential is always held in check by a "fearful asymmetry" that comes about when people with power seek to impose their will on others.[3]

This chapter proceeds in the same way as the last. It starts by describing who Orwell was and how people have tended to read his work. Then it shifts perspective to bring about a parallax view. After

2 All page numbers in this chapter's in-text citations come from the critical edition edited by Irving Howe, *Orwell's* Nineteen Eighty-Four: *Text, Sources, Criticism.* *Nineteen Eighty-Four* is in the public domain in some jurisdictions, including Canada, where the full text is available on the website of the Gutenberg project, http://gutenberg.ca/ebooks/orwellg-nineteeneightyfour/orwellg-nineteeneightyfour-oo-h.html.

3 Tomislav Z. Longinović, "Fearful Asymmetries: A Manifesto of Cultural Translation," 6.

it misreads *Nineteen Eighty-Four*, it shifts once more. All is not lost, and in the places where the novel goes beyond its appendix, we come to see that the power of surveillance and violence is not as absolute as it appears.

George Orwell and *Nineteen Eighty-Four*

George Orwell was the pen name of Eric Blair, who was born in 1903 and died in 1950. He was a prolific essayist and novelist and a harsh critic of totalitarianism and socialism, especially as it was being institutionalized in Europe after the Second World War. As a writer, he was known for his straightforward style and avoidance of "dying metaphors," "pretentious diction," and "meaningless words," as he explained in his essay "Politics and the English Language."[4]

Orwell is best known for his novels *Animal Farm*, a parable about animals who overthrow their human masters only to become human themselves, and *Nineteen Eighty-Four*, about everyman Winston Smith and his struggles against a state ruled by the Party and led by a figurehead called Big Brother. It was published in 1949, as "British capitalism was indeed merging with socialism under the guidance of Fabian social planners, and was doing so as welfarism."[5] It introduced an enduring set of ideas about language and government, such as the Thought Police (the all-powerful enforcers of orthodoxy who caused people to live "in the assumption that every sound you made was overheard, and, except in darkness, every movement scrutinized" [4]) and doublethink (the practice of holding "simultaneously two opinions which canceled out, knowing them to be contradictory and believing both of them" [25]).

The story *Nineteen Eighty-Four* tells is part romance, part thriller, part morality tale. Winston Smith lives in the oppressive super-state of Oceania, one of three that control virtually the whole world. The

4 George Orwell, "Politics and the English Language," 251–52.
5 Simon During, "More Orwell."

other two are Eurasia and Eastasia. Oceania includes most of the English-speaking world along with South America, while Eurasia includes Europe and the northern parts of the former Soviet Union, and Eastasia includes the southern parts of the Soviet Union along with China, India, and Pakistan. They are in a perpetual state of war, although alliances often shift. The war is unwinnable, and its real purpose, as Winston learns, is to provide social stability and structure by creating clear categories of *us* and *them*.

Oceania is ruled by the Party. Its elite members—the Inner Party—make up about 2 percent of the population. Its non-elite members—the Outer Party—make up about 13 percent. Non-members—the proles—make up the remaining 85 percent. The Party administers the government through four ministries. The Ministry of Truth produces the lies that allow the Party to maintain its power. (It also produces the saccharine pop songs and tawdry books that pacify the proles.) The Ministry of Peace runs Oceania's endless war, first with Eurasia, later with Eastasia. The Ministry of Plenty oversees rationing. Finally, the Ministry of Love tortures anyone who resists the will of the Party.

Winston rebels against the Party with his lover Julia. They are both Outer Party members, and they ally themselves with O'Brien, "a large, burly man with a thick neck and a coarse, humorous, brutal face [who] had a trick of resettling his spectacles on his nose which was curiously disarming" (9). He is an Inner Party member who claims to be part of the Brotherhood, a resistance movement ostensibly led by a disgraced Party leader, but in fact he is loyal to the Party. His invitation to Winston and Julia is a trap. Winston and Julia never know if the Brotherhood really exists, or whether it was just a rumour O'Brien used to lure them in. When Winston is incarcerated in the Ministry of Love, O'Brien is his torturer, and he causes Winston to betray his love for Julia. The book ends with Winston sitting in a café, shedding tears of joy because he has finally overcome his resistance to the Party. Just as an assassin's bullet—which O'Brien promised him would come—enters his brain, "Two gin-scented tears trickled down the sides of his nose. But it was all right, everything was all right, the struggle was finished. He had won the victory over himself. He loved Big Brother" (197). In that respect, *Nineteen Eighty-Four* is like Orwell's other novels that end with their "alienated heroes losing their individuality and being reconciled to the social order."[6]

Interpretations of *Nineteen Eighty-Four*

How have readers interpreted *Nineteen Eighty-Four*? The story is rich enough for many to find in it warnings about their own political circumstances. It is not hard, for instance, to find examples of doublethink in the words of the politicians one opposes. (Chapter 4 of this book describes how some Americans have interpreted Donald Trump's presidency through the lens of Orwell's book.)

The same was true of the book when it first appeared. Early reviewers debated whether it was satire, in the same vein as Jonathan Swift's *Gulliver's Travels*, a way to talk about the contemporary world that surrounded them. Some saw in its descriptions of London the wartime city they themselves had known only a few years before.[7] Reviewers who found themselves on the side of the political spectrum Orwell opposed saw something else altogether: rather than a critique of totalitarianism, they saw a defense of capitalism, leading one Communist reviewer to say the book "coincides perfectly with the propaganda of the National Association of Manufacturers."[8]

In the first decade or two after *Nineteen Eighty-Four* was published, a wide range of critics engaged with Orwell and his work. According to Simon During, "Lionel Trilling, Q. D. Leavis, Richard Hoggart,

---

6 During, "More Orwell."

7 See, for instance, the reviews collected in Howe, *Orwell's Nineteen Eighty-Four*, 291–97.

8 Samuel Sillen, "Maggot-of-the-Month," 299.

Richard Rorty, and even (with reservations) the young Raymond Williams, praised him." But Orwell has been "neglected," During writes, since the 1970s.[9] The aspects of his work that have continued to attract interest relate to language and good writing. Composition and rhetoric scholars, not to mention scholars of political communication, have focused in particular on the idea of "doublespeak," an invented word made by combining two other invented words, *Newspeak* and *doublethink*, which they use to mean

> language which makes the bad seem good, something negative appear positive, something unpleasant appear attractive, or at least tolerable. It is language which avoids or shifts responsibility; language which is at variance with its real and purposed meaning; language which conceals or prevents thought.[10]

Others note that Orwell's philosophy of language, as described in *Nineteen Eighty-Four* and "Politics and the English Language," is divided between a laudable search for plain-spoken clarity and a nostalgia for the past, "a conservatism that sometimes comes close to sentimentality."[11] (It's not clear whether the clarity Orwell sought ever existed or could exist, even within the bounds he himself tries to establish.)

"The Principles of Newspeak" as Translation Manual

If this is how people have interpreted *Nineteen Eighty-Four*, how do we generate a parallax view to see the same book from a new angle, one that places its parts in a different relation to each other? We

---

9 During, "More Orwell."

10 William Lutz, "Notes Toward a Definition of Doublespeak," 4. The rest of *Beyond Nineteen Eighty-Four*—a volume that Lutz edited and from which his essay comes— explores similar themes. Note that the word *doublespeak* does not appear in *Nineteen Eighty-Four*.

11 Walker Gibson, "Truisms Are True: Orwell's View of Language," 13.

focus on the appendix, "The Principles of Newspeak," rather than on the novel itself.

It's tacked onto the end of the novel, which mentions it only in passing with a note early in the first chapter that says, "Newspeak was the official language of Oceania. For an account of its structure and etymology, see Appendix" (5). It seems peripheral in that the story the novel tells is complete without it. But readers familiar with translation studies, if they look closely, will see in the appendix a description of different modes of translation, much like more conventional works of scholarship.[12] If we focus our attention there, the story becomes an illustration of a philosophy of translation put into practice.[13]

Newspeak, as the appendix explains, "was the official language of Oceania and had been devised to meet the ideological needs of Ingsoc, or English Socialism," and its purpose was "not only to provide a medium of expression for the world-view and mental habits proper to the devotees of Ingsoc, but to make all other modes of thought impossible" (198). It had identifiable means, goals, and effects. It functioned by substituting one word for many (means) as a way to restrict thought (goals) and cut people off from old ways of speaking and thinking (effects). The Party even employed a cadre of translators "engaged in producing garbled versions—definitive texts, they were called—of poems [and other texts] which had become ideologically offensive but which for one reason or another were to be retained in the anthologies" (29–30). Thus to see the appendix as a translation manual is not terribly farfetched.

The words devised for Newspeak (and thus the translation tools available to members of the Party) were divided into three

---

12 For instance, Antoine Berman, "Translation and the Trials of the Foreign."

13 Some of the few people to start with "The Principles of Newspeak" as a lens through which to interpret Nineteen Eighty-Four are the writers and producers of a 2017 stage adaptation. They observe that the appendix is "a really radical gesture against the rest of the book. It's a book about how you can't trust the written word." Quoted in Jennifer Shuessler, "With '1984' on Broadway, Thoughtcrime Hits the Big Time."

categories or vocabularies. The first, the A vocabulary, consisted of "the words needed for the business of everyday life," generally those "involving concrete objects or physical actions" related to eating, working, getting around, and so on (199). The second, the B vocabulary, consisted of compound words "which had been deliberately constructed for political purposes" (200). This category included the words most closely associated with *Nineteen Eighty-Four*, such as *Newspeak, doublethink, thoughtcrime,* and so on. Finally, the C vocabulary included "scientific and technical terms" (203), although not in the sense we might recognize today. Like the words in the B vocabulary, they were ideological: they "were constructed from the same roots [as the scientific terms we know now], but the usual care was taken to define them rigidly and strip them of undesirable meanings" (203). Technicians had access to the words they needed to do their work, but they had little knowledge of other branches of what we would recognize as science. In fact, science as a form of inquiry into the external world was simply inconceivable: "There was, indeed, no word for 'Science,' any meaning that it could possible bear being already sufficiently covered by the word *Ingsoc*" (203).

As one of the architects of the language (a character named Syme) explains to Winston, his job was not to create words but to destroy them:

> It's a beautiful thing, the destruction of words. Of course the great wastage is in the verbs and adjectives, but there are hundreds of nouns that can be got rid of as well. It isn't only the synonyms; there are also the antonyms. After all, what justification is there for a word which is simply the opposite of some other word? A word contains its opposite in itself. Take "good," for instance. If you have a word like "good," what need is there for a word like "bad"? "Ungood" will do just as well—better, because it's an exact opposite, which the other is not. Or again, if you want a stronger version of "good," what sense is there in having a whole string of

vague useless words like "excellent" and "splendid" and all the rest of them? "Plusgood" covers the meaning, or "doubleplusgood" if you want something stronger still. (35–36)

The appendix spells out this logic even more explicitly (199–200). To negate a word, a speaker added the prefix *un-*. To emphasize it, a speaker added *plus-* or, for still more emphasis, *doubleplus-*. Speakers could combine prefixes (making *doubleplusun-* an emphatic negation), as well as add suffixes such as *-wise*, to turn words into adverbs, and *-ful*, to turn them into adjectives. Nouns could also be used as verbs. Combined with the restriction of meanings to ideologically correct ideas, this logic made it possible to substitute one word for many. *Goodthink* (meaning "orthodox," "orthodoxy," "thinking in an orthodox way," etc.) and its derivatives (*ungoodthink*, etc.), could take the place of the class of words related to emotions (figure 14), which were politically dangerous in so far as they were unruly and hard to control (200–203).

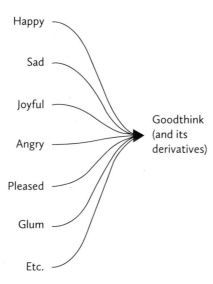

Figure 14. Translation of emotion words into variations of *goodthink*.

The Goals and Effects of Translation into Newspeak

The goal of Newspeak was to make ideas unthinkable by depriving people of the words they needed to think them. Newspeak's architects (as dreamt up by Orwell) observed that without language, people would experience the world around them as a meaningless flux, a jumble of impressions and sensations. Language imposed order by imposing meaning. Words carved the world up into discrete units.

Anyone who has learned a second language will grasp this idea intuitively: sometimes there's a word in your new language that simply doesn't translate back into your old. The units carved out by your new language are too different. An internet search for "words that don't translate to English," for instance, yields lists that tell you things like *dépaysement* is French for "the disorientation felt in a foreign country or culture, the sense of being a fish out of water."[14]

The linguists Edward Sapir and Benjamin Lee Whorf developed this hypothesis—that language structures how we see the world—in the 1920s and 30s.[15] Sapir, for instance, wrote,

> It is quite an illusion to imagine that one adjusts to reality essentially without the use of language and that language is merely an incidental means of solving specific problems of communication or reflection. The fact of the matter is that the "real world" is to a large extent unconsciously built up on the language habits of the group. No two languages are ever sufficiently similar to be considered as representing the same social reality. The worlds in which different societies live are distinct worlds, not merely the same world with different labels attached.[16]

Whorf went still further:

14 Dan Dalton, "14 Perfect French Words and Phrases We Need in English."

15 Whorf was Sapir's student. Although Sapir's influence on Whorf is clear, they did not in fact write any articles together, and much of what people recognize as the Sapir-Whorf hypothesis is an extrapolation from their respective publications.

16 Edward Sapir, "The Status of Linguistics as a Science," 209.

Language is not merely a reproducing instrument for voicing ideas but rather is itself the shaper of ideas, the program and guide for the individual's mental activity, for [her or] his analysis of impressions, for [her or] his synthesis of [her or] his mental stock in trade.[17]

If we take this assertion as a strong hypothesis, the implications are clear: to control how people think, it is enough to cut them off from their accustomed ways of speaking. (We can also take the Sapir-Whorf hypothesis in a weak form, too, where we identify exceptions and counterexamples. We will return to the weak form later in this chapter.) The architects of Newspeak wanted to make speaking a reflex, like when a doctor taps your knee and your leg jerks forward: "Ultimately," Orwell writes, "it was hoped to make articulate speech issue from the larynx without involving the higher brain centers at all. This aim was frankly admitted in the Newspeak word *duckspeak*, meaning 'to quack like a duck'" (203).

In short, in *Nineteen Eighty-Four*, Newspeak is effective because it cuts people off from their history and deprives them of their ability to make sense of the world themselves. Think back to the discussion of interpretants in chapter 1. People hear a word, and it makes them think of an idea, which reminds them of another, which reminds them of still another, and so on. Newspeak cuts people off from those interpretants. It substitutes the interpretants the Party wants, or, if somehow speakers achieve the "ideal"—such as it is—of duckspeak, it eliminates interpretants altogether (figure 15). In other words, Newspeak, along with the violence inflicted on people who rebel, helps create the conditions for a form of collective solipsism. If people can't trust their interpretations of the world or their recollection of history (on which they might base interpretations of the world), then the Party can interpret the world for them. O'Brien makes this state of affairs clear in a long exchange with Winston as he tortures

17 Benjamin Lee Whorf, "Science and Linguistics," [6]. See also Lutz, "Notes Toward a Definition of Doublespeak," 2.

him. Winston says that the world is older than the Party, and O'Brien tells him to prove it. Winston can't because he has no independently verifiable evidence. O'Brien (not to mention the Party he represents) claims that whatever Winston remembers, he remembers it wrong. Even if he had physical evidence, O'Brien would claim it was phony, a claim Winston could not refute. (If he tried to refute it, what evidence would he have?) As O'Brien says,

> We control matter because we control the mind. Reality is inside the skull. You will learn by degrees, Winston. There is nothing that we could not do. Invisibility, levitation—anything. I could float off this floor like a soap bubble if I wished to. I do not wish to, because the Party does not wish it. (176)

Through torture, O'Brien deprives Winston of any grounds on which he might stake a contradictory claim, just as the Party, through its institutionalized violence and surveillance, does to the people of Oceania. Through Newspeak, the Party deprives them of the very tools they would need to imagine that there might be a different way to know the world. Violence and language work together as complementary means of control.

Figure 15. A speaker of Newspeak succumbs to collective solipsism as they cease to trust their own interpretation of a sign. Drawn by author.

Solipsism

At this point, it would appear that cultural translation can be short-circuited. Its potential comes from the gap between what one person says and another person hears and understands, a gap brought about by the play of interpretants. If language and violence can cut people off from those interpretants, the potential for change will go unrealized.

In other words, we're 180 degrees away from where we were at the end of chapter 1. To find our path back, it is necessary to look more closely at the philosophy (or more precisely, the epistemological stance) of solipsism, whose name derives from the Latin words *solus*, meaning "alone," and *ipse*, meaning "self." As O'Brien tortures Winston, Winston wants to object to the "belief that nothing exists outside your own mind" (177). He searches for the name of this idea, which O'Brien gives him: "The word you are trying to think of is solipsism. But you are mistaken. This is not solipsism. Collective solipsism, if you like. But that is a different thing; in fact, the opposite thing" (177).

What exactly is this idea? Think of the movie *The Matrix*.[18] In the beginning, the hero, a computer programmer named Neo, is living a normal life, although he is puzzled by things that keep repeating themselves. He is contacted by a man named Morpheus, who offers him a choice. If Neo wants to understand the anomalies, he can swallow a red pill, although Morpheus warns him that if he does,

---

18 Lana Wachowski and Lilly Wachowski, dirs., *The Matrix* (1999). The conceit that makes *The Matrix* work, namely, that computers can create worlds that seem self-sufficient to the people inside their programs, is common in popular culture, revealing a range of different ways to think about solipsism. Fans of the 1990s program *Star Trek: The Next Generation* will recognize it in the episode "Ship in a Bottle," where a self-aware holographic "person" believes he exits the holodeck when really his consciousness is uploaded to yet another program. Fans of the more recent series *Black Mirror* will recognize it in a number of episodes, including "San Junipero," where the hero uploads her consciousness to a computer-generated island paradise.

he will face consequences he cannot yet grasp. If he wants to avoid those consequences, he can take a blue pill and return to his life. Neo takes the red pill, of course. (If he didn't, there'd be no plot.) He is then dragged violently out of his world, and he awakes to find himself in a womb-like pod with electrodes plugged into his brain. Everything he has experienced up to that point was in the matrix, a computer-generated world that felt real because his mind treated it as real. Now he is in a much harsher world, which gives him the perspective to see that the matrix simply provided him with a powerful illusion.

The matrix was a solipsistic world, existing (for him) only in his mind. Neo was made to imagine it.[19] It's the idea of being made to imagine that O'Brien has in mind when he says collective solipsism is not the same thing as solipsism. Collective solipsism is imposed from the outside, and it's more insidious because it causes people to doubt their senses and memory. How does the Party implement its strategies on a large scale? How does it create and control a *collective* form of solipsism? It uses techniques such as gaslighting, or "psychologically manipulat[ing] a person into questioning their own sanity," often by telling them that something they remember is not true.[20] The Party has an entire apparatus to do just that, including the Ministry of Truth, where Winston works, which is devoted to changing "historical" records to match the narrative of the day. The people of Oceania trust the narrative they are given more than their own memories or perceptions, to the point where it comes to replace their memories. Early in the book, for instance, Winston hears that chocolate rations are being reduced from thirty grams to twenty. He

19 Of course, how do we know that the "real" world Neo enters after he takes the red pill is any more real than the one he left behind?

20 American Dialect Society, quoted in Ben Yagoda, "How Old Is 'Gaslighting'?" The term comes from a film called *Gaslight* released in 1944, which was based on a play produced in 1938. It is about a man who tries to undermine his wife's confidence in her own perception by insisting that the gaslights in their house do not flicker, even though they do.

is called upon as part of his job to rewrite documents that showed that the ration had ever been thirty grams. The rewriting is so successful that a day later he hears that

> there had even been demonstrations to thank Big Brother for raising the chocolate ration to twenty grams a week. And only yesterday, he reflected, it had been announced that the ration was to be *reduced* to twenty grams a week. Was it possible that they could swallow that, after only twenty-four hours? Yes, they swallowed it. (40)

More dramatically, at a climactic point in the story, Oceania's war with Eurasia—its enemy up to that point—becomes an alliance, and its alliance with Eastasia turns into a war. Everyone is gathered for the public execution of Eurasian prisoners when, "at just this moment it had been announced that Oceania was not after all at war with Eurasia. Oceania was at war with Eastasia. Eurasia was an ally" (120). This statement contradicts everything people see around them. All the propaganda says the Eurasia is the enemy, but the Party's gaslighting is so efficient that the only possible response is the idea that they have been tricked: "The banners and posters with which the square was decorated were all wrong! Quite half of them had the wrong faces on them. It was sabotage! The agents of Goldstein [a traitor to the Party and ostensible leader of the Brotherhood resistance movement] had been at work!" (120).

In short, the Ministry of Truth treats history as a palimpsest, or a document (such as a medieval scroll) whose text is scraped off so the page can be used again. It constantly erases and rewrites the historical record, which has already been erased and rewritten often enough that the word *historical* is nonsensical. The record bears no relation to events that have actually happened, but in the Party's gaslit collective solipsism, those events don't matter. In fact, those events don't exist. The only ones that matter are those that matter to the Party: "In no case would it have been possible, once the deed [of fabricating the historical record] was done, to prove that any falsification had taken place" (28).

Where does all of this—Newspeak, torture, solipsism, gaslighting, and the palimpsest of history—leave the question of translation? "The Principles of Newspeak" ends by quoting the first lines of the U.S. Declaration of Independence ("We hold these truths to be self-evident, that all men are created equal, that they are endowed by their Creator with certain inalienable rights, that among these are life, liberty and the pursuit of happiness"). Then it explains,

> It would have been quite impossible to render this into Newspeak while keeping to the sense of the original. The nearest one could come to doing so would be to swallow the whole passage up in the single word *crimethink*. A full translation could only be an ideological translation, whereby [Thomas] Jefferson's words would be changed into a panegyric on absolute government. (205)

In other words, translation from Oldspeak (English as we speak it now) into Newspeak brings about a complete transformation of sense and reveals the limits of substituting one set of words for another when the words come from languages characterized by disjunctive worldviews.

The Lived Contradictions of Newspeak

This is the point where Orwell's explicit reflection on language stops but where the novel itself goes further. It provides certain clues about Newspeak in actual use, which is far more complicated than the appendix might lead us to believe. Linguistic reduction might work hand-in-hand with historical amnesia, but its effectiveness is not absolute. Orwell offers an important caveat: Newspeak would render "heretical thought" unthinkable only "so far as thought is dependent on words" (198). This caveat hints at the fact that, in some instances, thought is *not* dependent on words. Here is where we revisit the Sapir-Whorf hypothesis in a weak form, one that allows for the possibility of thought outside of language: although language does impose a way to interpret the world, it is not ironclad. The example I gave of a word with no equivalent in English—*dépaysement*—helps us understand the room we have to manoeuvre. I used English—despite its lack of a word!—to explain the concept in ways that helped you understand it. If a strong version of the Sapir-Whorf hypothesis held true, we would not be able to think outside the structure imposed by our language at all.

So how do we do it? In *Nineteen Eighty-Four*, characters think outside the structures of Newspeak in at least three ways. First, they engage in doublethink (the ability to treat two contradictory thoughts as true at the same time). Second, and more interestingly, they react to nonverbal signs, such as smells or sounds in nature. Finally, they encounter complex signs (those that are more than simple words) multiple times, and the signs evoke different things each time. In other words, characters are reflexive about their own thoughts. They are not as cut off from their history as the book would lead us to believe.

Doublethink

Throughout *Nineteen Eighty-Four*, Orwell repeats the same cryptic trio of aphorisms:

WAR IS PEACE

FREEDOM IS SLAVERY

IGNORANCE IS STRENGTH

At first glance, these translations (which is what they are, as *peace* replaces *war*, *slavery* replaces *freedom*, and *strength* replaces *ignorance*) seem nonsensical. How could war be its opposite? Or freedom or ignorance? What they reveal, in fact, is that Newspeak is grounded in a contradiction, that of doublethink, or the act of knowing and forgetting at the same time (but also forgetting what you needed to forget, and then forgetting the act of forgetting). "Even to understand the word 'doublethink' involved the use of doublethink" because people had to forget they were doing it (25). This act is the contradiction that makes Newspeak possible: doublethink involves having thoughts that Newspeak would stamp out, but without doublethink, Newspeak could not exist.

What makes the aphorisms examples of doublethink? War is peace because Oceania's perpetual state of war with its neighbours allows the Party to maintain order, if not peace, within its borders. Freedom is slavery because, as O'Brien explains, "power is collective. The individual only has power in so far as he ceases to be an individual" (175), which is to say, in so far as he submits himself to slavery. Ignorance is strength because the Party remains strong so long as its individual members are kept in a state of ignorant servitude.[21] In a feat of acrobatic dialectical thinking, people have to forget that war is war, freedom is freedom, and ignorance is ignorance. But the negated term in the dialectic remains in latent form. If it disappeared completely, there would be no need for either the Ministry of Truth (which labours to impose the Party's ideological apparatus) or the Ministry of Love (which serves as its repressive apparatus).

Nonverbal Signs

Other signs reveal something different about the caveat about language. They are nonverbal—sounds, sights, smells, or other sensations that evoke something for characters, even if the characters struggle to name what it is. The taste of real chocolate, rather than the "dull-brown crumbly stuff that tasted . . . like the smoke of a rubbish fire," stirs up for Winston "some memory which he could not pin down, but which was powerful and troubling" (81). Later, when

---

21 Much of this philosophy is laid out in *The Theory and Practice of Oligarchical Collectivism*, a book-within-a-book signed by Emmanuel Goldstein, the figurehead of the Brotherhood resistance movement. (O'Brien reveals when he tortures Winston that he is actually the author.) See 122–33.

he is awaiting his torturers, hunger evokes visceral notions of pain or panic, depending on how intensely he experiences it (152).

What makes these signs dangerous to the Party is their unruliness: the interpretants they evoke are visceral, and language is inadequate to describe them. They risk escaping the Party's control. Consider the moment when Winston and Julia first meet, beyond the reach of the Party's surveillance (or so they believe). They are in a field with bushes and trees, and they hear a thrush who seems to sing for the pure joy of it: "The music went on and on, minute after minute, with astonishing variations, never once repeating itself, almost as though the bird were deliberately showing off its virtuosity" (82). Winston gives himself over to the performance: "by degrees the flood of music drove all speculations out of his mind. It was as though it were a kind of liquid stuff that poured all over him and got mixed up with the sunlight that filtered through the leaves. He stopped thinking and merely felt" (82). Later, the last time he and Julia are together before the Thought Police move in to arrest them, they revisit the scene:

> "Do you remember," he said, "the thrush that sang to us, that first day, at the edge of the wood?"
>
> "He wasn't singing to us," said Julia. "He was singing to please himself. Not even that. He was just singing."
>
> The birds sang, the proles sang, the Party did not sing. . . . Everywhere stood the same solid unconquerable figure [a prole woman Winston has seen before], made monstrous by work and childbearing, toiling from birth to death and still singing. Out of those mighty loins a race of conscious beings must one day come. You were the dead; theirs was the future. But you could share in that future if you kept alive the mind as they kept alive the body, and passed on the secret doctrine that two plus two make four. (147)

Julia insists the bird's song was without meaning. Winston finds meaning there nonetheless: it reminds him of the prole woman he has heard singing, and the singing itself signifies something like freedom (figure 16). Hence the fear the Party has of these signs, which is apparent in its attempts to stamp them out. "The terrible thing that the Party had done was to persuade you that mere impulses, mere feelings, were of no account, while at the same time robbing you of all power over the material world" (110). The Party can never take this persuasion for granted. It constantly has to resort to brute force to try to overcome the power of these signs. The amount of force it uses is in direct proportion to the power of these signs.

Figure 16. When Winston hears the thrush singing, he thinks of freedom. Image of bird adapted from Smit (1869, "Cichlopsis Leucogonys"). Source: Wikimedia Commons.

Signs That Evoke History

A third set of signs reveals in yet another way the limits of the Party's control over thought. In contrast to the nonverbal signs, which tended toward the simple and unmediated, these signs are complex. They share an important trait: Winston encounters them twice over the course of the book, and their meaning changes because of the repetition.

What makes these examples interesting is that it is O'Brien (and through him, the Party) who exploits the semiotic gap between one use and the next. He presents them to Winston as a way to bring him into the Party's solipsistic world. The first time Winston encounters each of these signs, they evoke ideas of freedom; the second time, frustration and hopelessness, as O'Brien turns the idea of freedom against itself. In the first example, Winston is at the Ministry of Truth when he comes across half a page of newsprint with a photo of men named Jones, Aaronson, and Rutherford. The Party's official history records them as traitors. They confessed to their crimes and were executed. But the photo makes it clear that they were somewhere else when their supposed crimes took place. It is historical evidence that proves they were forced to lie. Such evidence, Winston realizes, is "enough to blow the Party to atoms" (53).

Later, Winston sees the photo again. O'Brien shows it to him briefly and then withdraws it from his sight.

> "It exists!" [Winston] cried.
> "No," said O'Brien.
> He stepped across the room. There was a memory hole [where people put paper to be incinerated] in the opposite wall. O'Brien lifted the grating. Unseen, the frail slip of paper was whirling away on the current of warm air; it was vanishing in a flash of flame. O'Brien turned away from the wall.
> "Ashes," he said. "Not even identifiable ashes. Dust. It does not exist. It never existed."
> "But it did exist! It does exist! It exists in memory. I remember it. You remember it."
> "I do not remember it," said O'Brien. (164)

Winston recognizes O'Brien's reaction as doublethink. The photo that once meant hope now meant "deadly helplessness" (164).

The second sign is an entire conversation Winston and Julia have with O'Brien when he has tricked them into believing he belongs to the resistance. O'Brien tells them they will receive orders they do not understand, and he wants to know what they are willing to do (figure 17). Will they commit "murder" or "acts of sabotage which may cause the death of hundreds of innocent people"? Will they "betray [their] country to foreign powers"? Will they be willing "to cheat, to forge, to blackmail, to corrupt the minds of children, to distribute habit-forming drugs, to encourage prostitution, to disseminate venereal diseases," or even "to throw sulphuric acid in a child's face" if it would help weaken the Party? (114–15).

Figure 17. Winston tells O'Brien he will do terrible things to overcome Big Brother. Drawn by the author.

Yes, they answer. Their assent, as they see it and as O'Brien explains it, evokes a hope without hope, the idea that the future will be better, even if they will not know it. "There is no possibility that any perceptible change will happen within our own lifetime," O'Brien says. "We are the dead.[22] Our only true life is in the future" (117). Later, when O'Brien is torturing Winston, he plays a recording

---

22 This is the same phrase—"We are the dead"—that Winston uses when he thinks about how the proles (whom he has seen singing) might overcome the Party. Right before the Thought Police raid their room, Winston and Julia repeat the phrase again. It loses its messianic overtones and becomes quite literal when the Thought Police confirm in response, "You are the dead" (147).

of this conversation: right after Winston accuses the Party of cruelty, O'Brien makes him listen to the terrible things he said he would do. A conversation that evoked notions of sacrifice in the name of freedom now evokes duplicity and moral depravity (figure 18).

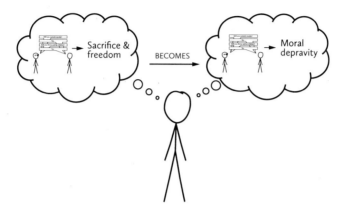

Figure 18. The conversation between Winston and O'Brien takes on a new meaning for Winston. Drawn by the author.

What do we learn from this example? The conversation itself does not change. Its second iteration is a recording, after all. O'Brien uses the repetition to attribute new meaning to it and break Winston's will. But there is something nonetheless redeeming about these examples, for they demonstrate that even the Party cannot change the fact that to use a sign is to transform it, and through that transformation, to translate it.

Conclusion: Cultural Translation Between Utopia and Dystopia

Chapter 1 presented a utopian vision of cultural translation: we can exploit the gap between signs to open up space for people who have been socially or politically excluded. This chapter presents the other side of the coin: we can also exploit this gap to close off space (the

Party told people whom to hate) and impose our will upon others through real and symbolic violence.

In this respect, *Nineteen Eighty-Four*, although fiction, provides a valuable lesson for the worlds we walk through every day. What should we make of the fact that people can see in it their current political situation? If anything, the book and the tension it illustrates (between things that can be controlled through violence and things that can't) help clarify the relationship between hope and work. Cultural translation has the potential to bring more openness to the world, but we must not let optimism overcome us. Similarly, cultural translation has the potential to allow for cruelty and injustice, but we must not let pessimism overcome us, either. Whatever effect is to be achieved, we must work to achieve it. We must actively engage with each other and with the systems of power that structure our relationships.

Hence the need for tactics to prompt others to see the world from a different perspective. Hence the question that grounds the next chapter: what tools do we have at our disposal to allow us to engage meaningfully with people with whom we do not see eye-to-eye?

Translational Invention,
Inventive Translation

The preceding chapters have taken a bird's-eye view of cultural translation. Chapter 1 described the utopian dreams it inspires. Chapter 2 described the dystopian nightmares. Where does that leave us?

This chapter looks at the nuts and bolts of cultural translation. What techniques do people use to change other people's minds—to induce them to see the world through a parallax view? In that respect, it changes the scale of our analysis from macro to micro. Through this act of refocusing, we will see that both the utopian and dystopian views are misleading if they overlook the contingent nature of cultural translation, which is not inherently good or bad. It is a tool, and its value depends on the use to which we put it.

Consider the point where the last chapter left off. The world of *Nineteen Eighty-Four* is hermetically sealed, turned in on itself in a form of (nearly) inescapable solipsism. It might remind us of our current political circumstances, but our world is not as bleak as Winston Smith's.[1] Of course, we don't live in some magical world where everyone gets along, either. Instead, we're somewhere in between.

---

1 I write this sentence with the idea that although my present as writer and your present as reader are not the same, something about your current political situation

Still, the worlds we live in are more closed than we think. They differ from *Nineteen Eighty-Four* in degree more than substance. What I mean is that we impose symbolic order on our experience in the form of explanations about what the world is and how it operates. We recognize certain phenomena as causes and others as effects, building a chain of events that lets us explain who we are and what we are doing. We create, both individually and in interaction with others, symbolic worlds that appear complete and self-sufficient.

These worlds lead us to a rather pedestrian form of solipsism (as I hinted at in the opening lines of the introductory chapter). We don't hold hard and fast to the idea that nothing outside our mind exists, but, pragmatically speaking, we act as if that were the case. We struggle to make sense of new ideas because they don't follow the logic that appears to us to be common sense. We're faced with a paradox that researchers in science education identified nearly four decades ago: "Whenever the learner encounters a new phenomenon, [she or] he must rely on [her or] his current concepts to organize [her or] his investigation."[2] In other words, we stack the epistemological deck: to understand something new, we have to use the conceptual tools we've already developed to investigate it. The effect is counterintuitive. New ideas leave our conceptual foundations untouched: rather than challenge our a priori assumptions, they strengthen them.

Another way to see this paradox is to recognize that the symbolic worlds we inhabit can always absorb evidence that, to an outside observer, appears to contradict our views. Consider one controversial issue in our era of polarized politics—climate change. People on opposite sides of the spectrum arrive at different interpretations of major weather events, which fit into their narratives about politics and climate in ways that support the ideas they already have. In 2016,

will remind you—as my current situation reminds me—of *Nineteen Eighty-Four*.

2 George J. Posner, Kenneth A. Strike, Peter W. Hewson, and William A. Gertzog, "Accommodation of a Scientific Conception: Toward a Theory of Conceptual Change," 212.

for instance, a fire engulfed the town of Fort McMurray, Alberta, the centre of bitumen oil production in Canada. The year leading up to the fire had been dry, a fact that prompted some to think climate change was responsible for the conditions that made the fire possible. Others blamed cyclical weather patterns. But however obvious the role of climate change was to people who believed in it, they could make no argument that would change the minds of those who did not. Indeed, skeptics had a ready-made explanation for any "evidence" about climate change they might present: it was political theatre and victim-blaming, especially if they suggested that oil production contributed to the dry weather.[3] Not only could skeptics explain away evidence by attributing it to politics, but doing so seemed to confirm something they already knew (or thought they knew), namely that their opponents were crassly and shamelessly political (figure 19).[4]

Figure 19. Two people with competing frames for understanding the 2016 Fort McMurray forest fires. Drawn by the author.

3 Martine Danielle Stevens, "Ultradeep: A Critical Discourse Analysis of Fort McMurray and the Fires of Climate Change." As Stevens points out, of course, it is hard to draw a direct causal link between climate change and specific weather events. But what matters for this example is the way people perceived a link.

4 For other examples, see Kyle Conway, Little Mosque on the Prairie *and the Paradoxes of Cultural Translation*, 27–30.

But, of course, people *do* change their minds. We don't dismiss every new idea: sometimes the external world intrudes into our internal solipsisms, and sometimes new ideas cause us to step back and examine how we understand things. Maybe they hit upon some inconsistency in our worldview—something we can't explain but can't necessarily put our finger on—or maybe they're simply too provocative to ignore. People change their minds about global warming, for instance, when they see its effects as personal, rather than politically motivated. In series of surveys between 2011 and 2015, more than 20 percent of respondents who had changed their mind about global warming said they did so because they had personally experienced the impact of climate change.[5] A *New York Times* article from 2018 described how a handful of people saw past their skepticism: a meteorologist spoke directly with scientists, a coal miner saw the effects of his career on the environment around him, a community organizer in Miami saw the threat higher waters posed for her neighbourhood.[6] In each case, people came to see the effects of climate change in light of their own experiences, where they made a different kind of sense. They found a different frame for making sense of the world, which caused them to interpret evidence such as rising waters or increased average temperature in a new way (figure 20).

What pins can we use to prick our solipsistic bubbles? Poetry is one. It can bring about a "meditative state of mind" that "yields clarity" about "the way our voices sound when we dip below the decibel level of politics."[7] Humour is another. Jokes work by saying two things at once. They have two meanings—one literal or denotative, the other ironic or connotative—that contradict each other. The

5 Kathryn S. Deeg, Erik Lyon, Anthony Leiserowitz, Edward Maibach, John Kotcher and Jennifer Marlon. "Who Is Changing Their Mind About Global Warming and Why?"

6 Livia Albeck-Ripka, "How Six Americans Changed Their Minds About Global Warming."

7 Tracy K. Smith, quoted in Ruth Franklin, "Tracy K. Smith, America's Poet Laureate, Is a Woman with a Mission."

contradiction makes us laugh and see the world differently, at least for the brief moment where we hold the two meanings together.[8]

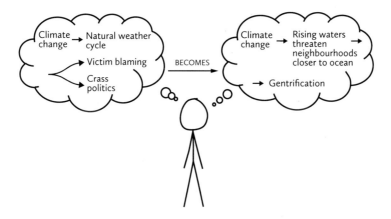

Figure 20. A climate change skeptic comes to interpret climate change as a threat to her neighbourhood rather than a result of the natural weather cycle when she sees it through a personalized frame. Drawn by the author.

This chapter focuses on yet another pin—that of shock—used by a Russian artist named Petr Pavlenskii.[9] He is known for performances, which he calls "actions," that involve inflicting pain upon his body in protest against injustices perpetrated by the Russian government. This chapter examines his actions through the lens of rhetorical invention, which, drawing on Aristotle, I described in chapter 1 as the ability to generate arguments by identifying and using "the available means of persuasion" in any given situation (*Rhetoric*, I.2).[10]

---

8 Conway, Little Mosque on the Prairie *and the Paradoxes of Cultural Translation*.

9 The artist's name is transliterated from the Cyrillic spelling, *Пётр Павленский*, a number of different ways. I have adopted the spelling used in *Russia—Art Resistance and the Conservative-Authoritarian Zeitgeist*, edited by Lena Jonson and Andrei Erofeev, which is the source of the translation of the dialogue on which I focus at the end of the chapter.

10 All quotations in this chapter come from the translation of *Rhetoric* by W. Rhys Roberts, in the digital edition published by the MIT Internet Classics Archive. Citations refer to book (Roman numerals) and part (Arabic numerals).

Invention, like many ideas in this book, has paradoxical qualities. On the one hand, any act of invention is contingent on context. On the other, at least as laid out by Aristotle, the tools of persuasion (of which invention is one), are formulaic, which is the opposite of contingent. After an overview of invention and the paradox it engenders, this chapter turns to Pavlenskii's art. It describes the art world's interpretations of his actions and then asks what happens if instead we look at them through the lens of rhetorical invention. Then it identifies ways his actions prompt viewers (not to mention his police interrogator) to see the world from a new angle. He uses two rhetorical tools: he implicates his viewers in his actions, and he compels them to see his actions in the context of a different interpretive frame, replacing one, whether legal or psychological, with another from the world of symbols and art.

Aristotle and Rhetorical Invention

Aristotle was a list-maker who lived in the fourth century BCE and was a student of Plato's. He wrote about biology, physics, language, art, and poetry, among other things, working systematically through categories of objects and ideas, cataloguing their relationships to one another.

In *Rhetoric*, he explores the nature of persuasion and speech-making. He makes a list of tools a speaker (or "orator" or "rhetor") can learn to use to persuade different types of people in a variety of situations. He categorizes these tools as a function of how they relate to what speakers want to accomplish, how they craft their

Note that *invention* is, as I wrote in the introductory chapter, one of those terms that might strike contemporary readers as odd: why this term and not another? Aristotle answers that question when he writes that there are two modes of persuasion, one that uses "such things as are not supplied by the speaker but are there at the outset—witnesses, evidence given under torture, written contracts, and so on," the other that uses such things "as we can ourselves construct by means of the principles of rhetoric. The one kind has merely to be used, the other has to be invented" (I.2).

appeals, and what their listeners expect, given their life experience. The first, and arguably the most powerful, of these tools is invention, a term that, for Aristotle, refers to the construction or generation of arguments. These tools require no specialized skills, only the desire to acquire them (I.2). Anyone studying *Rhetoric*, Aristotle says, can learn this system and become a persuasive speaker.

Aristotle begins by identifying three types of speeches, political, forensic, and ceremonial, based on what speakers want to accomplish. Sometimes an orator seeks to persuade others about the future (as in the making of laws, when legislators want to shape how people will behave), sometimes about the past (as in court, when judges want to know what an accused person has done), sometimes about the present (as in situations meant to honour someone, when a rhetor uses a speech about a person to talk about the current situation more broadly) (I.3). Similarly, he identifies three modes of persuasion. Speakers are persuasive when they appear trustworthy (an appeal to *ethos*), when they influence how listeners feel (*pathos*), and when they present cogent, evidence-based arguments (*logos*). These tools all work in tandem. Appeals to emotion are made all the stronger when they come from someone who appears trustworthy, just as they are stronger when they accompany appeals to reason.

He breaks each of these modes down further. With respect to character or ethos he says, "It adds much to an orator's influence that his own character should look right and that he should be thought to entertain the right feelings towards his hearers" (II.1). In other words, speakers are persuasive when they appear trustworthy and authoritative. They control their vocal tone, physical gestures, and other aspects of delivery to appear prudent and virtuous. (Think of someone about whom you might say, "That person has real presence." They walk into a room and command attention by virtue of the way they carry themselves and address their listeners. Those actions that contribute to that person's presence, so to speak, constitute the appeal to ethos.)

Aristotle is also concerned with the character of the listeners (which is his way of talking about what they find persuasive): as much as speakers should "entertain the right feelings" toward their listeners, they should also work to put their listeners "in just the right frame of mind" toward them (II.1). They can learn techniques to this end, based for instance on the age and wealth of the listeners, along with their station in life. Aristotle thinks speakers should appeal to a man's desire and frame their appeals to address the roots of that desire.[11] Young men, he says, are hot-headed and love honour and victory because they want to feel superior. Speakers can appeal to them by linking what they want them to think or do to the honour they might achieve if they do it (II.12). Conversely, old men, having been tricked and cheated many times, act carefully, and they want only what they need to keep on living, rather than honour or victory. Speakers can persuade them by appealing to their sense of prudence (II.13). To be fair, two millennia later, we might take issue with Aristotle's essentialism, but his insight into the relationship between desire and persuasion is valuable nonetheless.

With respect to emotion or pathos, he speaks of influencing "those feelings that so change men as to affect their judgements, and that are also attended by pain or pleasure" (II.1). Emotions act on people in different ways and can thus be put to different use. Anger, which Aristotle defines as a desire for revenge in the face of injustice, is effective for persuading judges to convict someone accused of a crime (II.2). Fear, which he defines as pain in the face of imminent danger, is effective for persuading people to act in a way that promises them safety (II.5).

With respect to reason or *logos*, Aristotle describes two types of appeal: examples (a form of induction) and enthymemes (a form of deduction). Rhetorical examples are a type of comparison where, to persuade listeners about a given situation, speakers compare it to one that is already familiar, in hopes that listeners draw the

---

11 Aristotle envisions listeners as men.

same conclusion about the new situation as they would about the old.[12] Enthymemes are a type of syllogism, or a logical statements made up of two parts, namely a major premise (such as a categorical statement: "All people are mortal") and a minor premise (such as a statement of contingent fact: "You are a person") that, when both are true, allow us to arrive at a conclusion (the implications of the major and minor premises: "You are mortal"). What makes an enthymeme different from a typical syllogism is that the speaker doesn't state all the propositions: "For if any of these propositions is a familiar fact, there is no need even to mention it; the hearer adds it himself" (I.2). The speaker lets the listener fill in the gaps. (If I say "you are a person and therefore mortal," I do not need to include the premise that all people are mortal. You would arrive at my intended conclusion because you already know people are mortal.)

This overview is necessarily brief. Rhetorical invention encompasses a wide range of strategies and tools to address an equally wide range of situations. Aristotle provides many more tools, such as a catalogue of propositions "about greatness or smallness and the greater or the lesser—propositions both universal and particular [that make it possible] to say which is the greater or lesser good, the greater or lesser act of justice or injustice; and so on" (I.3). He also catalogues common arguments in his work called *Topics* and explores emotion in *On the Art of Poetry*, his treatise on poetics. And he is not the only person to study invention. It held philosophers' and scholars' interest before Aristotle (whose *Rhetoric* was in part a response to Plato) and after (Cicero explores it in *On Invention*), and it continues to hold their interest now.

---

12 Sometimes when my kids are arguing over something they both want, I say to them, "Remember the last time you couldn't share? What happened then? You got in a fight and both had to spend time in your rooms. You know what's going to happen if you keep up the argument you're just starting now?" That's an example in Aristotle's sense. I'm comparing their current argument to one they've already had in hopes that their memory of the consequences then will persuade them to change their behaviour now. (Rarely does this happen.)

In light of the idea's rich history, what this chapter does is rather modest: it identifies and explores one inventional tool, cultural translation, to see its value in a specific type of circumstance. Our task is to see how invention becomes a pin with which to prick our solipsistic bubbles. The point is not to use translation to say something new about invention, but to use invention to say something new about translation. In other words, the idea of invention provides us a new view on the work of translation.

Like Aristotle, we need to identify the available means of persuasion. For that, we turn to Russian performance artist Petr Pavlenskii and consider both his art and what he says about it. Pavlenskii takes pains (literally and figuratively) to put members of his audience into "a right state of mind," as Aristotle would say. His performances or "actions" evoke a strong visceral reaction, on which he builds an argument when he talks about them later in the media, in court, and in police interrogation. His central strategy—and the tool that is our focus—consists in leading a listener to interpret a contested idea in the context of a competing conceptual frame, as in the examples earlier about global warming, where people came to see weather events through a personal frame. More simply, he helps people see things in a new way through a parallax view.

Now it is time to break his acts of invention down into their constituent parts.

The Art of Petr Pavlenskii

Petr Pavlenskii is a Russian performance artist best known for inflicting pain on himself in protest against the abuses of the Russian government. In 2012, for instance, in an action called *Seam* (*Шов*), he sewed his lips together in front of the Kazan Cathedral in St. Petersburg to protest the trial of the punk band Pussy Riot, whose members had been arrested after a performance they staged in Moscow's Cathedral of Christ the Saviour. In 2013, in an action called *Carcass* (*Туша*), he wrapped himself naked in barbed wire to protest laws restricting individual freedoms. Perhaps his best known action, *Fixation* (*Фиксация*), took place in 2013, when he nailed his scrotum to the paving stones in Moscow's Red Square as "a metaphor of the apathy and political indifference and fatalism of the modern Russian society."[13] And in 2014, in an action called *Segregation* (*Отделение*), he climbed up on a wall outside the Serbsky Centre, a psychiatric hospital in which political prisoners from the former Soviet Union disappeared, and cut off part of his earlobe (figure 21). Not all of his actions involve self-mutilation, however. In 2014, in *Freedom* (*Свобода*), he set a barricade of tires on fire on the Malyi Konyushennyi Bridge in St. Petersburg to evoke anti-Russia protests in Kiev, and in 2015, in *Threat* (*Угроза*), he set the doors to the headquarters of Russia's secret police (formerly the KGB) on fire.

Figure 21. Petr Pavlenskii performs *Segregation*, 2014. Photograph by Missoksana, CC-BY-SA 4.0. Source: Wikimedia Commons.

---

13 Pavlenskii, quoted in Craig Stewart Walker, "Madness, Dissidence and Transduction," 694.

Members of the art world have reacted to Pavlenskii in a variety of ways, but all take it as given that his actions are indeed art. Critics reacting to *Fixation* saw it as "the final argument that can be made in an ongoing dispute with the government," as an expression of "the poetic language of performance to a highly effective political end," or, in a different vein, as an act that was ultimately derivative of the "various forms [of self-mutilation] by members of the Wiener Aktionismus movement back in the 1960s."[14] They also placed him in the context of past artists, such as van Gogh (who famously cut off his ear), and prior artistic movements, such as the Russian Futurists (who rejected traditional notions of art as they explored the machines of modern life in the 1910s) and the Viennese Actionists (who engaged in violent performance art in the 1960s), as noted above.[15] They saw Pavlenskii's immediate predecessors as the band Pussy Riot, not least because he held a sign referring to their incarceration in his action *Seam*. (For his part, Pavlenskii has rejected most suggestions about his artistic lineage, citing only Chris Burden, an American artist who once had an assistant shoot him in the arm, as an inspiration.)[16]

Others interpreted Pavlenskii's actions through different frames, or the "principles of organization which govern events—at least our social ones—and our subjective involvement in them," to borrow a definition from Erving Goffman.[17] Less abstractly, they give different answers to the question, "What is it that's going on here?"[18] Artists

14 In order, Marat Guelman, David Thorp, and Anton Nossik, quoted in Ekow Eshun, Maryam Omidi, Jamie Rann, and Igor Zinatulin, "The Naked Truth: The Art World Reacts to Pyotr Pavlensky's Red Square Protest."

15 Per-Arne Bodin, "Petr Pevlenskii and His Actions," 271–78; Amy Bryzgel, "Chopped Earlobes and the Long History of Political Shock Art in Russia"; Ingrid Nordgaard, "Documenting/Performing the Vulnerable Body: Pain and Agency in Works by Boris Mikhailov and Petr Pavlensky"; and Walker, "Madness, Dissidence and Transduction."

16 Bodin, "Petr Pavlenskii and His Actions," 272.

17 Erving Goffman, *Frame Analysis: An Essay on the Organization of Experience*, 10–11.

18 Ibid., 8.

debated the newness of Pavlenskii's work. Other people, especially members of the public or actors in Russia's legal system, thought his self-mutilation could be only a symptom of mental illness. Others in the legal system saw his actions as vandalism or desecration of Russia's patrimony, both of which were crimes (see table 1).

Table 1. Different frames used to explain Petr Pavlenskii's actions

Frame	Interpreter	Interpretation
Artistic	Critics	Pavlenskii's actions, whether original or derivative, are art.
Psychiatric	Members of public Actors in legal system	Self-mutilation is a symptom of mental illness, so Pavlenskii must be ill.
Legal	Actors in legal system	Pavlenskii's actions constitute an act of vandalism or desecration and are crimes.

How can we understand the concept of frames in the theoretical terms set out in previous chapters? Charles Peirce, whose notion of "interpretant" grounds the analysis in chapter 1 and thus forms the foundation of this book, classifies a sign as a function of three conditions: what makes something a sign, how it relates to its referents (that is, what it's a sign *for*), and what it reveals about them. He also classifies signs as a function of their complexity. The simplest signs ("firsts") are unmediated and unreflexive; more complex signs ("seconds") are mediated, but not yet reflexive; the most complex signs ("thirds") are both mediated and reflexive, and they derive from convention, habit, or law.[19] The simplest signs are ones where the three conditions are all firsts, such as "a nebulous patch of color, seeing a blotch of red in an afterimage, hearing the wind blow

19 Charles Peirce, *The Philosophy of Peirce: Selected Writings*, 98–119.

through an old house, the musty smell while walking in a forest, the aftertaste from a deliciously exotic meal."[20] The most complex are ones where the three conditions are all thirds: the "paradigm case is that of an inference of an argument, which shows the connection between one set of propositions (the premises) and another (the conclusion)."[21] As a simple sign evokes an interpretant (which in turn evokes another and another and another), it becomes a building block for signs that are more complex. A nebulous patch of colour becomes the colour red, which people recognize in different contexts, and in certain contexts it takes on specific meanings: if people are driving and see a red octagon, for example, they know to stop.

Or, in the case of Pavlenskii, the feeling of resistance becomes an awareness of politics and history, and his actions come to evoke a series of propositions. Self-mutilation is a symptom of mental illness, and Pavlenskii mutilates himself, so he must be ill. Or vandalism is a crime, and Pavlenskii's actions are a form of vandalism, so the police and courts are right to treat him as a criminal.

In this way, we can use the way signs grow in complexity to understand the idea of a frame. When people see Pavlenskii's actions, they have an initial reaction as to what those actions are—*what it is that is going on here*, to paraphrase Goffman. That initial reaction then shapes the chain of interpretants that leads to their conclusions about the meaning of his actions. It directs the movement from one interpretant to another, so that someone watching or reading about an action arrives at one of many potential conclusions, to the exclusion of the others. That initial reaction—the first interpretant—becomes the frame.[22] Pavlenskii replaces that first interpretant—the primary

20 James Jakób Liszka, *A General Introduction to the Semeiotic of Charles Sanders Peirce*, 48.

21 Ibid., 52.

22 It is first in a conceptual sense, in that it is primary, rather than a strictly chronological sense, although in some circumstances it might be both. I'm taking liberties with Goffman here. He doesn't necessarily see frames as something people actively shape, but I do. That idea comes more from media studies, where people like

frame—with another interpretant and changes not just the chain of associations but the final conclusions at which people arrive. In other words (there is that telling phrase again!), his strategy is to perform an act of cultural translation.

This idea of a frame-as-first-interpretant makes it possible to see Pavlenskii's actions from a new angle, not just as art but also as rhetorical invention. Consider his response to the psychiatric frame. Many people see his actions and think he must have a mental illness. Their logic goes something like this: self-mutilation is so grotesque that is must be a symptom of mental illness (their major premise). Pavlenskii engages in self-mutilation (their minor premise). Therefore he must be mentally ill (their conclusion) (figure 22).[23]

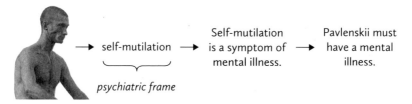

Figure 22. A psychiatric frame used to interpret Pavlenskii's *Segregation*. Adapted from photograph by Missoksana, CC-BY-SA 4.0. Source: Wikimedia Commons.

Pavlenskii refutes this syllogism by challenging its major premise: people do the things he has done for other reasons, such as to criticize an oppressive government. He shows that his purpose is critique by engaging with the court system in strategic ways. He insists on being charged with the most serious crime, even when prosecutors would prefer lesser charges, effectively forcing their hand. He puts them in the position of making arguments they don't want to

---

Robert Entman have used frames to talk about the choices journalists make when they draw attention to certain aspects of a story. See Robert M. Entman, "Framing: Toward Clarification of a Fractured Paradigm."

23 Cf. Walker, "Madness, Dissidence and Transduction."

make, confronting them with a forced choice: either they support the system at the cost of their integrity, or they maintain their integrity and challenge an unjust system.[24] This approach suggests a type of methodical thought that is not a symptom of mental illness. Thus Pavlenskii establishes a competing syllogism: self-mutilation can be something other than a symptom of mental illness (his major premise). He hurts himself, but for reasons related to art and protest (his minor premise). Therefore his actions are not a sign of mental illness (his conclusion) (figure 23).[25]

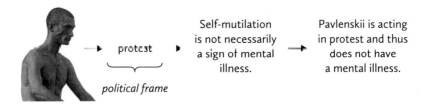

Figure 23. A political frame used to interpret Pavlenskii's *Segregation.* Adapted from photograph by Missoksana, CC-BY-SA 4.0. Source: Wikimedia Commons.

Pavlenskii takes a similar approach to the legal frame. Police officers, lawyers, and judges tend to see his actions as crimes. Their logic follows these lines: people who destroy property that is not theirs commit acts of hooliganism, vandalism, or desecration and should be charged with a crime (their major premise). Pavlenskii has committed such acts, such as when he lit tires on fire on the bridge in

24 Bodin, "Petr Pavlenskii and His Actions."

25 Strictly speaking, the syllogisms here do not hold up to a rigorous logic. The major and minor premises of Pavlenskii's syllogism, for instance, do not lead necessarily to the conclusion (mental illness does not stop people from being politically active, for instance). What matters discursively, however, is the conclusion he leads viewers to make (see, for example, Bodin, "Petr Pavlenskii and His Actions"). This idea is consistent with Aristotle's account of *logos*, which depends on "the proof, *or apparent proof*, provided by the words of the speech itself" (*Rhetoric*, I.2, emphasis added).

St. Petersburg (their minor premise). Therefore he should be charged with a crime (their conclusion) (figure 24). Not surprisingly, those charges have been the ones he has faced: hooliganism, a charge also brought against Pussy Riot for their protest in the Cathedral of Christ the Saviour, and vandalism or desecration, a charge applied when a person vandalizes cultural artefacts.[26]

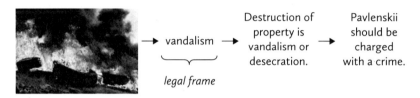

Figure 24. A legal frame used to interpret Pavlenskii's *Freedom.* Adapted from photograph by Mstyslav Chernov (Kiev, 18 February 2014), CC-BY-SA 3.0. Source: Wikimedia Commons.

Pavlenskii employs a similar strategy to challenge this frame as he does to challenge the psychiatric frame: he implicates his viewers, especially those in law enforcement, in his actions. He wants them to see they are cogs in a machine: "People in law enforcement agencies are forced to become tools," he says; "everything human in them is suppressed. But many of them doubt that what they are doing is right, so the human element can rebel against the functional one."[27] He establishes a different syllogism: the legal system turns people

---

26 Walker, "Madness, Dissidence and Transduction," 691; and Bodin, "Petr Pevlenskii and His Actions," 277. The term *desecration* reveals another dimension of the legal frame, namely, its relation to the religious sphere. In some cases, the link is direct: Pussy Riot protested in a cathedral, and Pavlenskii's action *Seam*, where he expressed support for Pussy Riot, took place in front of a different cathedral. Elsewhere it is indirect, as when art critics point out "the resemblance of his performances to the public behaviour of Russian fools for Christ, which included provocations directed at the powers that be, nakedness and extreme asceticism" (Bodin, "Petr Pevlenskii and His Actions," 277).

27 Quoted in Ivan Nechepurenko, "How Russia's 'Most Controversial Artist' Persuaded His Interrogator to Change Sides."

into cogs or tools (his major premise). Police officers enforce the law (his minor premise). Therefore they are tools, people who must surrender to the system (his conclusion). He also establishes a second syllogism, where the conclusion of the first is the minor premise: people who are tools in the system want to regain their humanity (major premise). Police officers are tools (minor premise). Therefore they want to regain their humanity (conclusion), which they can do, he suggests, by seeing his actions as art, rather than hooliganism or vandalism (figure 25).

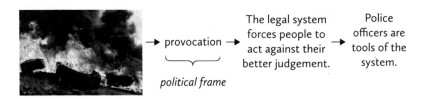

Figure 25. A political frame used to interpret Pavlenskii's *Freedom*. Adapted from the photograph by Mstyslav Chernov (Kiev, 18 February 2014), CC-BY-SA 3.0. Source: Wikimedia Commons.

Freedom and "A Dialogue about Art"

We have seen how Pavlenskii replaces one frame with another at the level of his art in society. But what about at an interpersonal level? What are the strategies he uses in conversation to prompt someone to see the world from a new perspective? After *Freedom* in 2014, when he set fire to a pile of tires on a bridge in St. Petersburg, he was arrested and interrogated. Unbeknownst to his interrogator, Pavel Yasman, he recorded the interrogation. He later published a transcript on the website Snob.ru.[28] An English translation was

---

28 Lena De Winne, "*Допрос Петра Павленского. Пьеса в трех действиях* [The Interrogation of Petr Pavlenskii: A Play in Three Acts]."

published in 2017.[29] The interrogation, which took place in three sessions, was published in the form of a dialogue between Pavlenskii and Yasman, and it reveals the artist's rhetorical strategies. Remarkably, when the interrogation was done, Yasman quit his job to become a human-rights lawyer, having been persuaded by Pavlenskii to examine his life more closely.[30]

Throughout the interrogation, Pavlenskii and Yasman argue from within identifiable, incompatible frames—Yasman's legal, Pavlenskii's symbolic. At various points, they both try to argue from within the frame of the other. Pavlenskii finally prevails by showing Yasman where the contradictions lie within the legal frame and how Yasman perpetuates those contradictions, which ultimately are contrary to his own personal convictions.

Yasman's main strategy is to focus the discussion as narrowly as possible. He does not want to consider context: he wants to talk about specific acts, namely those related to the fire. He constantly chides Pavlenskii "not [to] think so globally in such matters" (284). His logic follows these lines. His major premise is that "we have laws and a legislature that describes specific actions for which a person is legally responsible" (281). His minor premise is that Pavlenskii committed one of these acts by lighting the tires on fire: "It does not matter whether it is art or not art" (282). His conclusion is that Pavlenskii is legally responsible and must suffer the consequences.

In several places, Yasman tries to argue from within Pavlenskii's symbolic frame. He offers examples of art (as he imagines it) where the actions that matter are clearly crimes. "But you might just go and murder someone for the sake of art" (279). Or "let's say that some people go to the grave of an African-American, [and they] break the tombstone, smash it, but play it in a theatrical way" (280).

29 Petr Pavlenskii and Pavel Yasman, "A Dialogue About Art." For the sake of legibility, in this section I give the page numbers referring to this transcript in parenthetical in-text citations.

30 Nechepurenko, "How Russia's 'Most Controversial Artist' Persuaded His Interrogator to Change Sides."

Pavlenskii responds by showing either how these acts are unprincipled and not art or how context matters: "It could be the friends of the African-American [who break the tombstone]," he says, "because their country's ritual provides for some kind special treatment. As in Tibet, for example" (280).

Such responses derive from Pavlenskii's symbolic frame. He adopts a broad view: "The act of art occurs in the symbolic field for the most part; and to a certain extent, of course, in reality. That is, we must begin to look at the action from different angles" (283). Symbolism and law, he argues, are largely incompatible. With respect to the specific charges of desecration he faces, he says:

> I will try to talk about vandalism from a legal point of view. Like talking about desecration. What is desecration? A humiliation of something: piss, crap, smash, this can be seen as desecration, because some actions are well-established symbols of humiliation from the point of view of the amassed experience. But fire is not a symbol of humiliation. (286)

He establishes yet another syllogism: Desecration implies humiliation (major premise). Or, to restate it, if there is no humiliation, there is no desecration. That, he maintains, is his case: the fire he set put no one at risk, did not harm the bridge, and evoked social struggles in support of freedom. "The bridge was not humiliated" (288) (minor premise). Therefore he committed no crime (conclusion).

Pavlenskii goes a step further by showing Yasman how Yasman has been instrumentalized within a dehumanizing system. At the beginning of the third session, he asks why Yasman has returned. Yasman answers, "I . . . got my ass handed to me because the case is still in court" (288). Yasman says he has to carry out his instructions. "So you admit that you are a tool," Pavlenskii responds:

> This instrumentalization, the power just instrumentalizes people. . . . [These systems] make you do what you do not want

to do. They take people who are initially able to recognize art, to make art. And then some people are forced to attack others. (288)

Pavlenskii is critiquing a system that makes people act against their will. Yasman recognizes himself within that system because he feels constrained in the way Pavlenskii describes. In effect, Pavlenskii has introduced a new syllogism. A dehumanizing system must be challenged (major premise). Yasman sees the Russian legal system as dehumanizing (minor premise). It no longer provides an explanation of the world he finds convincing, and it must be challenged (conclusion). The last words of the interrogation are Yasman's: "I'm going to leave the system sooner or later," he admits. "I just don't know how" (291).

Conclusion: What Invention Teaches Us About Translation

Throughout the interrogation, Pavlenskii's appeals to reason are clear. Major premise, minor premise, conclusion. Major premise, minor premise, conclusion. He also works to put Yasman "in just the right frame of mind," as Aristotle suggests (*Rhetoric*, II.1), by acting in such a way that his words are imbued with authority (although, of course, we have only a translated transcript to go by). He is unwavering in his insistence that Yasman consider the broader context, but he never says a rude word. When Yasman tries to provoke him, he responds with restraint, while Yasman often appears flustered. And Pavlenskii appeals to those "feelings that so change men as to affect their judgements" (II.1), specifically Yasman's sense of frustration in the face of a dehumanizing system and his hope in light of the choices he can make to escape that system. In short, he is inventive in Aristotle's sense: he has used identifiable tools to generate an argument tailored to a specific person and circumstance.

What does his approach reveal about translation—that is, the substitution of signs? Pavlenskii was successful when he changed his interrogator's initial interpretant—the first thing he thought of when he considered the tires Pavlenskii set on fire. When Yasman's first thought was *dehumanizing system* rather than *law-enforcement*, the final conclusion at which he arrived was different. He changed his mind about Pavlenskii because Pavlenskii's actions came to have a more personal meaning for him, much as the climate change skeptics in the introduction changed their mind when extreme weather events touched them personally.

In this way, translation becomes a tool for invention. It's at our disposal as one possible way to persuade the person we're talking to. At the same time, the idea of invention—the ability to see and use the tools at hand—helps us see translation as strategic. Pavlenskii's approach of implicating his viewers to prompt them to see his actions in a different frame is one such strategy.

These strategies, of course, are not the only ones, nor is change of this type a foregone conclusion. At the macro, conceptual level, cultural translation had utopian and dystopian possibilities, as we saw in chapters 1 and 2. The same is true at the micro, strategic level, as this chapter has shown and the next chapter shows.

Fake News and
Perspective Unmoored

There's a pattern to this book. Chapters 1, 2, and 3 all explore the same phenomenon, but on different scales and with different polarities (some look at positive examples, while some look at negative).

Chapter 1 argues that all communication is translation because words never mean exactly the same thing twice. That is, a word evokes something different for listeners from one use to the next, if only because when I use a word and you, in your response, use it too, you have to account not only for *your* use of the word, but also for *mine* (which I didn't need to do). We can make use of this semiotic gap to perform acts of cultural translation and, if we're strategic, help people see the world from a new perspective, making it a tool against the oppression of others. Chapter 2 presents the flip-side of chapter 1. It is concerned with ways cultural translation can stop people from seeing the world from any perspective at all. People can exploit the gap between uses of a word to cut others off from their own inter-pretation of the world, thus depriving them of the tools they need to make their own decisions. This is what O'Brien does to Winston in *Nineteen Eighty-Four*. Chapter 3 makes the same argument as chapter 1, but on a micro-scale. It looks at tactics people can use to change others' minds by changing their initial interpretive frame. It highlights an approach taken by performance artist Petr Pavlenskii, who implicates the people he's talking to in the argument he's making. The shock people experience in recognizing themselves in his argument prompts them to see the world anew, as if through a parallax view: the objects they're looking at don't move, but they as observers do, causing them to see the objects in a new configuration.

Chapter 4, which is about fake news, follows this pattern. Like chapter 2, it is about perspective unmoored, in ways similar to what we saw in *Nineteen Eighty-Four*: after the election of Donald Trump as president of the United States in 2016, the idea of fake news in a "post-truth" society reminded so many people of Orwell's book that it became a surprise best-seller.[1] Like chapter 3, it is about tactics, in ways similar to what we saw in Pavlenskii's art: the act of implicating people in an argument can cause them to reject new perspectives just as easily as adopt them.

Fake news is a complex topic, which this chapter explores by placing debates about it in two contexts: first, ideas of objectivity in journalism, philosophy, and science, and, second, past controversies about the status of facts in reporting. It then examines the tactics used by President Trump to tether the phrase *fake news* to a new set of ideas. The central question is this: how has the term *fake news* evolved? Its meaning—as previous chapters would lead us to expect—has not remained stable from one use to the next. In the years leading up to the 2016 election, it usually referred to fake news *programs*, such as those that aired on the U.S. cable network Comedy Central. Immediately after the election, journalists from broad-circulation outlets such as the *New York Times* talked about fake news as stories that were false. Trump (not to mention authoritarian leaders around the world) then co-opted the term, stripping it of its critical edge by applying it to

---

1 Michiko Kakutani, "Why '1984' Is a 2017 Must-Read."

stories he found troublesome.[2] What's striking about the shift is the degree to which Trump's use of the term has caused a collective sense of crisis among journalists. What tactics has Trump used, and why did they generate this sense of crisis? In short, how did this change in meaning take place, and what made it stick?

What Is Objectivity?

Perhaps it goes without saying, but to function as informed citizens in a democracy, we need to know what's going on in the world around us. We need to talk with others to identify problems and explore possible solutions. We need to argue, and ideally we do so with some belief in the notion that we can trust that what we think is true is in fact true. We want to be sure we're making the right choices or advocating for the best course of action.[3]

But we can't know the world merely as it is. We know it through our senses, first of all, which act as mediators between us and the things we experience. We have no independent way to verify that what our senses tell us is true—to do so, we'd have to gather information about the world yet again through the mediation of our senses. In other words, we have no choice but to rely on our senses, which might deceive us.

There's also a lot of world that we'll never personally experience. I've lived quite a few places (in eleven cities in three countries on two continents), and I speak two languages. Many people have seen much more than I have. But none of us, not even the most experienced

2 In a tweet from May 2018, Trump made the link between "fakeness" and negative coverage clear: "Just reported that, despite the tremendous success we are having with the economy & all things else, 91% of the Network News about me is negative (Fake)." Quoted in Tamara Keith, "President Trump's Description of What's 'Fake' Is Expanding."

3 Or so I stubbornly believe. I became a teacher based on this stubborn belief. Call me naïve if you will, but this is a fight I refuse to give up.

world-travellers, will ever see any more than a miniscule percentage of what's out there. So we must rely on the accounts of others, many of whom we'll meet only through TV or the internet. We must trust them if we are to have any confidence in what they show us.

Here is where the idea of objectivity comes into play. In a philosophical sense, objectivity is the capacity to describe the world as it is, rather than how we perceive it to be. We achieve objectivity to the degree that we remove our own subjective perspective from the process of observation. In other words, an observation is objective if it's true regardless of who makes it. This task, of course, is paradoxical: we're trying to use our senses to overcome the limits imposed by our senses, as they mediate our contact with the world.[4]

Journalists have a different (but related) sense of objectivity. For them, it's a way to compensate for the perspective they bring to the events they describe. Journalists are constantly making choices about what makes an event newsworthy, or even what events constitute "news" in the first place. They write about some aspects of an event but not others, decisions that come from their personal and professional experience, which is in turn shaped by a history of social and economic pressures shaping the news industry. Although we might take ideas of objectivity for granted now, it's important to understand that they developed in specific places at specific times, namely the English-speaking world in the nineteenth and twentieth centuries. They are not universally shared or applied, as journalists in different places and traditions have differing priorities and habits. In fact, we can understand the skepticism many people now express

---

4 The philosophical approach that addresses this paradox head on is phenomenology. It consists in asking how we *experience* the world, rather than what the world *is*. Edmund Husserl, for instance, takes as his object of investigation not the thing he perceives—a person standing in front of him, for instance—but instead his experience of perception itself. See Husserl, *The Crisis of the European Sciences and Transcendental Phenomenology: An Introduction to Phenomenological Philosophy*. For a more contemporary account addressed to twenty-first century readers, see Samuel D. Rocha, *Folk Phenomenology: Education, Study, and the Human Person*.

about journalists' motivations and the veracity of their reporting by taking a closer look at this history.

Sociologist Jean Chalaby describes the development of professional notions of objectivity as part of a shift that English-language journalism underwent between the 1830s and the 1920s.[5] This shift came about because of reporters' access to new technologies and their development of new journalistic techniques. In the first case, the telegraph made it possible for them to write about things happening too far away to see in person. No longer did communication involve the movement of people (they didn't have to travel to where events took place) or of physical media such as written documents (they didn't have to rely on trains or other modes of transport to deliver accounts of faraway events).[6] In the second case, American journalists began to organize their reports around "fact-centred discursive practices."[7] One of their new tools was the interview, which became common practice in the 1860s.[8]

The shift that led to contemporary notions of objectivity related most importantly to the way newspapers were funded. Before the 1830s, newspapers were dependent on political parties and on the government for their funding. As printing technologies developed (for instance, with the introduction of steam-powered rotary presses in the mid-nineteenth century), the cost of production fell. Publishers could produce more copies and sell them for less. Their increased reach made them attractive to advertisers, who provided money to replace the revenue they had received from political parties. Advertisers wanted to reach the largest audience possible. In order not to alienate readers, reporters adopted a more politically neutral

5 Jean Chalaby, "Journalism as an Anglo-American Invention: A Comparison of the Development of French and Anglo-American Journalism, 1830s–1920s."

6 With respect to the role of the telegraph in changing how people related to space and distance, see James Carey, "Technology and Ideology: The Case of the Telegraph."

7 Chalaby, "Journalism as an Anglo-American Invention," 310.

8 Ibid., 312.

approach. This neutrality, borne of newspapers' increasing economic autonomy, came to define how journalists understood their professional obligations. *Objectivity* came to mean "political neutrality."[9]

The ways journalists put these ideas into practice were also shaped by social and economic factors. In the 1970s, sociologist Gaye Tuchman spent time in the northeastern United States among reporters going about their work. She observed that they treated objectivity as a way to mitigate risk. Specifically, they worried that they could be held legally accountable (through libel laws) if they wrote something false. To avoid that possibility, they adopted a set of professional practices meant to deflect accusations of bias. For instance, they presented conflicting explanations of events (that is, they covered "both" sides of a story). They also sought out and presented evidence that supported the assertions they made. When they wrote something controversial, they made "judicious" use of quotation marks (that is, they quoted someone making a controversial statement, rather than making it themselves). Finally, they structured their information in a conventional sequence, with the most important facts first, then the explanations of those facts later.[10] (This is the "inverted pyramid" approach, which grew out of the emphasis on facts Chalaby observed in the professional practices that developed in the nineteenth century.)

What this brief history reveals is one of the sources for people's current skepticism about journalists and their intentions. If objectivity in a philosophical sense is an illusion, and if objectivity in a journalistic sense is merely a practice, why *shouldn't* we be skeptical about how journalists pursue their work? We as news consumers are savvy about the social and economic factors that shape what

9 Ibid., 320. Of course, this reliance made a different type of influence possible: advertisers can also shape content, a fact that has become especially clear since the 1990s, when cable news networks, with the support of their advertisers, carved out new audiences by catering to specific political views.

10 Gaye Tuchman, "Objectivity as Strategic Ritual: An Examination of Newsmen's Notions of Objectivity."

journalists do. Politics in North American and European democracies have grown increasingly polarized, and it's not hard to find bias against our point of view, whichever it is, in different outlets. No one will deny that the world depicted by Fox News is not the same as the one depicted by National Public Radio, the Canadian Broadcasting Corporation, or the *New York Times*. So what's to say that the stories journalists present are in any way *true*?

Fake News: A Brief History

The multiplicity of different viewpoints to which people were exposed with the arrival of the internet, cable news, and social media, among other things, meant that habits journalists had long adopted under the label of objectivity no longer served to generate the trust they had in the 1970s. In other words, in the time leading up to and immediately following the 2016 U.S. election, Americans were ripe for the idea of fake news. They didn't trust journalists. More than half thought that the news media were biased, regardless of their political affiliation. More than three-quarters of Republicans didn't trust the media, conservative Republicans being the least likely of all to trust them. Democrats tended to trust them more, but not by much. The more they diverged from the centre, the less trustful they were (figure 26).[11]

If people distrusted the news media, they distrusted social media—where many false stories circulated—even more. Only 4 percent of "web-using U.S. adults" said they trusted information they got from social media "a lot," while another 30 percent said they trusted it "some."[12] This immense distrust translated into a situation where many people "[saw] fake news as different from poor journalism

11 Amy Mitchell et al., *The Modern News Consumer: News Attitudes and Practices in the Digital Era*, 9.

12 Ibid., 7. See also Richard Fletcher and Rasmus Kleis Nielsen, "People Don't Trust News Media—and This Is Key to the Global Misinformation Debate," 14–15.

primarily by degree."[13] The habits journalists had long adopted under the label of objectivity no longer served to generate the trust they had in the 1970s.

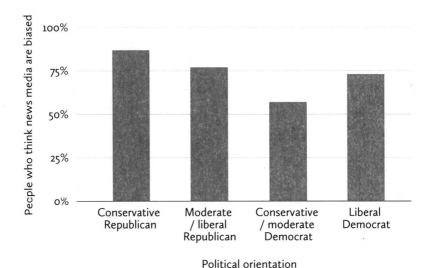

Figure 26. Percentage of people who think media are biased, as a function of political orientation. Data collected from Mitchell et al., 2016, *The Modern News Consumer*, 10.

Add to this the active efforts that professional internet trolls were making to spread disinformation, and the mix is potent. The Internet Research Agency, based in St. Petersburg, Russia, was the best-known organization, employing "hundreds of Russians to post pro-Kremlin propaganda online under fake identities, including on Twitter, in order to create the illusion of a massive army of supporters." It has been responsible for "highly coordinated disinformation campaign[s], involving dozens of fake accounts that posted hundreds of tweets for hours, targeting [lists] of figures precisely chosen to generate maximum attention."[14] Its activities have been well covered

---

13 Fletcher and Nielsen, "People Don't Trust News Media," 15.

14 Adrian Chen, "The Agency."

in the U.S. press, giving Americans even more reason to be skeptical about the news they read or see.

To be sure, the phenomenon of made-up stories is not new. Michael Schudson and Barbie Zelizer cite examples as far back as "anti-Semitic blood libel stories in 15th century Europe to church-supported missives of divine retribution following the 1755 Lisbon Earthquake."[15] They also quote Thomas Jefferson, who lamented in 1807 that "the man who never looks into a newspaper is better informed than he who reads them; inasmuch as he who knows nothing is nearer to the truth than he whose mind is filled with falsehoods & errors."[16]

The phrase *fake news* also shows up in greater and lesser frequency over the course of the twentieth and early twenty-first centuries, as this *n*-gram shows (figure 27). (An *n*-gram measures how often a word or phrase appears in a given corpus, or collection of texts. In this case, the corpus is all the books digitized by Google.)[17]

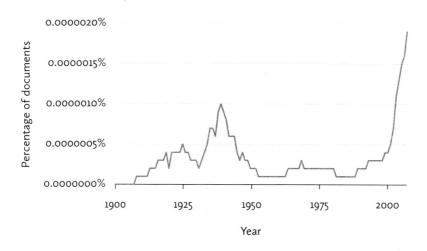

Figure 27. *N*-gram representing the use of the phrase "fake news," 1900–2008. Data collected from Google Books Ngram Viewer.

15 Michael Schudson and Barbie Zelizer, "Fake News in Context," 1.

16 Ibid.

17 Jean-Baptiste Michel et al., "Quantitative Analysis of Culture Using Millions of Digitized Books."

There are a number of peaks and valleys. One peak comes during the First World War, and another, steeper peak, during the Second World War. A third, subtler peak is observable in the 1960s and 1970s, during the Cold War. All three are indices of the concerns people in the English-speaking world had about propaganda (during the world wars) or Soviet *dezinformatsiya* (during the Cold War).[18]

The last peak, beginning in about 2000, reflects a different concern. As the cable industry in the United States became more competitive, with an ever-increasing number of channels dividing viewers into ever-smaller groups, networks had to find ways to distinguish themselves from their competitors. One network, Comedy Central, did so by creating satirical news programs such as *The Daily Show*, which began to air in 1996. Jon Stewart became the host in 1999, right before the contested presidential election of 2000, the 9/11 terrorist attacks, and the tumultuous presidency of George W. Bush. With Stewart as host, *The Daily Show* attracted many viewers, especially from younger demographics that were less likely to watch conventional news. It also produced spin-off shows such as *The Colbert Report*, a parody of conservative talk shows. Scholars, journalists, and other professional opinion-makers either worried about or celebrated the trend, especially as studies began to show that these programs could increase engagement among younger voters.[19]

Since the election of Donald Trump as president of the United States in 2016, interest in fake news—returning here to the older sense of "made up news"—has risen again. Figure 28 shows the search trends for the phrase "fake news" on Google from January 1, 2016, to July 16, 2018. (It shows the frequency of searches, broken down by week, as compared to the week when "fake news" was most searched. It reports the number of searches as a percentage of that peak.)

18 Schudson and Zelizer, "Fake News in Context," 2.

19 See, for example, Jody Baumgartner and Jonathan S. Morris, "The *Daily Show* Effect: Candidate Evaluations, Efficacy, and American Youth"; and Jeffrey P. Jones, *Entertaining Politics: Satiric Television and Political Engagement.*

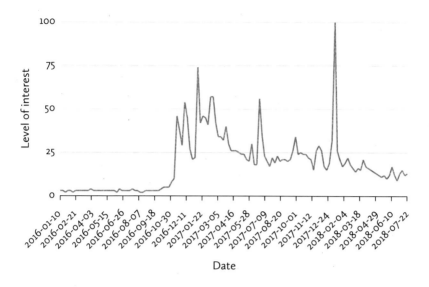

Figure 28. Google searches for "fake news" from January 2016–July 2018. Data collected from Google Trends.

Before November 2016, the month of the election, the rate of searches was relatively flat. The rate of searches picked up immediately after the election, peaking right after the inauguration during the week of January 8, 2017, with sustained but slowly declining interest for the next six months. It peaked again about a year later, during the week of January 14, 2018, when Trump made a show of awarding the "Fake News Awards."[20]

People's concerns about fake news have changed, especially since 2016. It became clear during the election that the technological environment, especially with social media, had changed dramatically even in comparison to the 2008 or 2012 elections. Technology has lowered the cost of production and allowed a wider range of media-producers to enter the market. Consequently, the conditions Tuchman described in the 1970s are no longer present. The journalists she described upheld practices of objectivity in part out of

20 See Jon Greenberg, Louis Jacobson, and Manuela Tobias, "Fact-Checking Donald Trump's Fake News Awards."

a sense of professionalism, but also in part out of fear of losing readers to their competitors. When the costs of entry were high, markets were limited, and if one organization lost a reader (for instance, if its reporters acted unprofessionally), its competitors likely gained a reader. Now the logic of competition is different: new competitors gain readers by rejecting the norms of the past in favour of provocation, thus "undermin[ing] the business models of traditional news sources that had enjoyed high levels of public trust and credibility."[21]

Social media have also played an important role in changing how people find and consume news. In 2016, about 40 percent of U.S. adults often got news online (through social media and other websites), while about 60 percent got it from TV. Younger people (between the ages of 18 and 29) were more than twice as likely than older people (above age 65) to get their news online (50 percent versus 20 percent).[22] Bots, or automated fake accounts, amplified the effects of sharing: "By one recent estimate—that classified accounts based on observable features such as sharing behavior, number of ties, and linguistic features—between 9 and 15% of active Twitter accounts are bots."[23] The effect on the circulation of fake news has been dramatic. Research published in *Science* found, "Falsehood diffused significantly farther, faster, deeper, and more broadly than the truth in all categories of information, and the effects were more pronounced for false political news than for false news about terrorism, natural disasters, science, urban legends, or financial information."[24]

What does this brief history tell us about fake news? It helps us see that it's not one thing. The term is polysemic (that is, it has many competing meanings—*polysemy* comes from the Greek πολυ, or *poly*,

21 David M. J. Lazer et al., "The Science of Fake News," 1094.

22 Mitchell et al., *Modern News Consumer*, 5.

23 Lazer et al., "Science of Fake News," 1095.

24 Soroush Vosoughi, Deb Roy, and Sinan Aral, "The Spread of True and False News Online," 1146.

"many" and σῆμα, or *sêma*, "sign"). Its meaning is contested, and some meanings that were once prominent (such as the reference to comedy news shows from the early 2000s) have lost their currency. In the context of the United States immediately after 2016, the meanings related to misinformation were the most important politically.[25] But something has happened in the time since then:

> This phrase has been irredeemably polarized in our current political and media climate. As politicians have implemented a political strategy of labeling news sources that do not support their positions as unreliable or fake news, whereas sources that support their positions are labeled reliable or not fake, the term has lost all connection to the actual veracity of the information presented, rendering it meaningless for use in academic classification.[26]

In other words, fake news has long been a feature of what we would now call the media environment. What makes it different now, according to Michael Schudson and Barbie Zelizer, is the anxiety it has produced about the professionalization of journalism, accompanied by a growing recognition among members of the public, as well as scholars and journalists, of the challenges of objectivity. Finally, what makes it different is also its propagation by politicians across the globe, especially the president of the United States.[27]

So how do we understand the shift in ideas evoked by the term, and, more to the point, the strategies employed by President Trump to bring about that shift?

---

25 Scholars have even broken down fake news into different types, depending on the degree to which authors mean to mislead, or the effects they hope to achieve. See Hossein Derakhshan and Claire Wardle, "Information Disorder: Definitions."

26 Vosoughi, Roy, and Aral, "Spread of True and False News Online," 1146.

27 Schudson and Zelizer, "Fake News in Context," 3.

Gaslighting

The same tools we developed in chapter 3 are useful here, in particular the idea of frames as elements of logical syllogisms (or fully developed signs, in Peirce's terms), which we used to explain how one person could prompt another to see the world from a new perspective. Here we will use frames too, but to look at an inverse case. They will help us identify one strategy Trump has used to make people doubt news sources that, in the past, employed the techniques identified by Tuchman and Chalaby to demonstrate their objectivity, or at least their neutrality. This doubt has played a key role in bringing about the shift in meaning of *fake news* that has alarmed journalists because of the way it has caused some readers' perspective to become unmoored.

Of course, Trump has used more than just one strategy. For one thing, he often simply makes bald assertions that journalists for outlets such CNN and the *New York Times* are peddling lies: "Don't believe the crap you see from these people, the fake news," he told a convention of the Veterans of Foreign Affairs in Missouri in July 2018. "What you're seeing and what you're reading is not what's happening."[28] His supporters have turned "fake news" into a chant they repeat at rallies. But one specific strategy interests us here: his technique, broadly speaking, of gaslighting (or denying things his listeners know to be true), or, narrowly speaking, of manufacturing situations where journalists he dislikes appear to contradict themselves.

Commentators across the political spectrum have noted Trump's habit of saying something and then denying it later. During the 2016 presidential campaign, the website Politifact catalogued "17 times Donald Trump said one thing and then denied it," including a claim he made—and then later forgot—about having one of the best memories in the world.[29] A staffer for Ted Cruz, Trump's principal rival for

28 Quoted in Katie Rogers and Maggie Haberman, "Spotting CNN on a TV Aboard Air Force One, Trump Rages Against Reality."

29 Linda Qiu, "17 Times Donald Trump Said One Thing and Then Denied It."

the Republican nomination in 2016, identified a pattern in Trump's approach. First, he makes a claim that people, especially in the media, are unlikely to accept, in order to create a "media frenzy." Second, he asks what *other* people are saying, as a way to attribute responsibility to someone else for saying controversial things. Third, he promises to produce evidence that will "get to the truth of the matter." Fourth, he attacks the character of his detractors and opponents. Fifth, and finally, he simply declares victory when he's ready to move on to a different topic.[30]

Rhetorical scholar Jennifer Mercieca gives a name to this approach. She identifies it as *paralipsis* (παράλειψις, from *para*, "beside" and *leipein*, "to leave"), a "device that enables [Trump] to publicly say things that he can later disavow—without ever having to take responsibility for his words."[31] It consists in quoting someone else, but then denying any responsibility for the claim that person is making. It gives Trump plausible deniability when he talks about controversial ideas: he can claim the ideas aren't his and he's only quoting someone else. Twitter is an especially apt platform for this approach, given the ease of retweeting someone else's post: "Trump can argue that he can't be held accountable because he wasn't the one who originally posted the tweet. He can shrug and claim that he's simply giving a voice to an idea."[32] He can benefit from the support of white supremacists, for example, by retweeting their posts, but he can also claim ignorance of their views when pressed by reporters.

The "Animals" Coming into the Country

This technique, in particular as it involves putting journalists in a position where they appear to violate their own professional norms,

---

30 Amanda Carpenter, *Gaslighting America: Why We Love It When Trump Lies to Us*, 15.

31 Jennifer Mercieca, "There's an Insidious Strategy Behind Donald Trump's Retweets."

32 Ibid.

is clear in a series of events that followed a controversial statement Trump made in May 2018. He was in California to talk about sanctuary cities, whose police officers limit their co-operation with federal officers who enforce immigration laws. They do so out of a concern to provide services to everyone, even those whose precarious immigration status might dissuade them from approaching the police for help. In that context, Fresno County Sheriff Margaret Mims raised concerns about the gang MS-13, which originated in Los Angeles in the 1980s and grew in strength in Honduras and El Salvador when its members were deported. Trump had frequently referred to the gang's excessive violence to justify his hardline stance on immigration. Mims wanted to talk about the limits she faced because of California's sanctuary laws.

The exchange was controversial because of Trump's response to Mims when she said that she couldn't contact ICE (the U.S. Immigration and Customs Enforcement) in certain circumstances, even if an MS-13 member were involved:

SHERIFF MIMS: There could be an MS-13 member I know about—if they don't reach a certain threshold, I cannot tell ICE about it.

THE PRESIDENT: We have people coming into the country, or trying to come in—and we're stopping a lot of them—but we're taking people out of the country. You wouldn't believe how bad these people are. These aren't people. These are animals. And we're taking them out of the country at a level and at a rate that's never happened before. And because of the weak laws, they come in fast, we get them, we release them, we get them again, we bring them out. It's crazy.[33]

Journalists, along with other public officials (and especially Democratic politicians), objected to the term *animals*, which they

33 "Remarks by President Trump at a California Sanctuary State Roundtable." Also quoted in Linda Qiu, "The Context Behind Trump's 'Animals' Comment."

thought Trump had applied broadly to immigrants coming into the United States. Trump and his defenders countered that *animals* referred narrowly to MS-13 members.

What mattered for both was what Trump meant by "people coming into the country." The two camps used different interpretive frames, with corresponding syllogisms, to make sense of his comments. The *New York Times* (on which I will focus here because it has been one of Trump's biggest critics and one of his most frequent targets) interpreted the comments within a historical frame, where Trump's past comments about immigrants, especially during the 2016 campaign, shaped how people understood his use of the word *animals*. Trump's administration, in contrast, interpreted his comments within a security frame, which was concerned more narrowly with a subset of immigrants, namely those who belonged to gangs.

The first article published by the *New York Times* opened by saying, "President Trump lashed out at undocumented immigrants during a White House meeting on Wednesday, warning in front of news cameras that dangerous people were clamoring to breach the country's borders and branding such people 'animals.'" In the next paragraph, it made the historical frame clear by explaining, "It was hardly the first time the president has spoken in racially fraught terms about immigrants."[34] Indeed, Trump declared in the speech announcing his candidacy for the presidency that "when Mexico sends its people, they're not sending their best. . . . They're sending people that have lots of problems, and they're bringing those problems with us. They're bringing drugs. They're bringing crime. They're rapists."[35] During his campaign, he had promised to strengthen immigration laws and even build a wall on the U.S.–Mexico border.

---

34 Julie Hirschfeld Davis, "Trump Calls Some Unauthorized Immigrants 'Animals' in Rant."

35 Donald Trump, "Here's Donald Trump's Presidential Announcement Speech."

The chain of interpretants suggested by this article (as well as articles that followed the next day) is illustrated in figure 29.[36]

recent history frame

Figure 29. Donald Trump's use of the word *animals* interpreted through the frame of recent history.

The initial sign (the word *animals*), as interpreted through the frame of recent history, evokes immigrants in a broad sense. That association in turn evokes a more complex sign, a syllogism according to which Trump has appealed to nativist tendencies in the past by making disparaging remarks about immigrants (major premise), and about whom he is making disparaging comments now (minor premise). Therefore he must be using the word *animals* in a broad sense, to appeal to the same nativist tendencies as before (conclusion). The idea that he is describing more than just MS-13 (as he would claim the next day) is suggested by the broader context of the roundtable, which was about sanctuary cities, where the threat of gangs was merely an example used to support Mims's claims. In fact, Linda Qiu, responding to Trump's supporters two days after the exchange, explained that Mims's complaints were true only of immigrants—whether gang members or not—who had not committed violent crimes. As soon as they committed a violent crime, they were no longer eligible for protection under sanctuary city laws.[37] The

---

36 The *New York Times* brought up the history frame again in an editorial about the Trump administration's policy of separating children from their parents, which it viewed as following logically from Trump's other expressions of animosity toward immigrants, going back to the early days of his campaign. See *New York Times* Editorial Board, "The Cruelty of Breaking Up Immigrant Families."

37 Qiu, "Context Behind Trump's 'Animals' Comment."

idea that Trump was referring only to violent MS-13 members was logically inconsistent: the limits Mims faced, to which Trump was responding, did not apply to MS-13.

The Trump administration, on the other hand, interpreted the "animal" comments through a different lens, that of security. The day after the roundtable, Trump sought to clarify his meaning, placing his comments in the context of the immediate exchange with Mims, rather than the roundtable itself: "I'm referring, and you know I'm referring, to the MS-13 gangs that are coming in. We have laws that are laughed at on immigration. So when the MS-13 comes in, when the other gang members come into our country, I refer to them as animals."[38] The word *animals*, he contended, referred only to MS-13 gang members, with the resulting syllogism looking like figure 30:

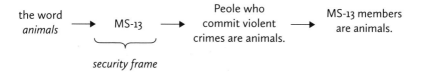

security frame

Figure 30. Donald Trump's use of the term *animals* as interpreted through the frame of security.

People who committed violent crimes were animals (major premise), and MS-13 members committed such crimes (minor premise). Therefore they—but not immigrants who were not violent—were animals (conclusion). On May 18, Trump's press secretary, Sarah Huckabee Sanders, made a similar point by describing violent acts committed by MS-13:

> It took an animal to stab a man a hundred times and decapitate him and rip his heart out. It took an animal to beat a woman— they were sex trafficking—with a bat 28 times, indenting part

38 Quoted in Julie Hirschfeld Davis and Niraj Chokshi, "Trump Defends 'Animals' Remark, Saying It Referred to MS-13 Gang Members."

of her body. And it took an animal to kidnap, drug and rape a 14-year-old Houston girl.[39]

The point here is not to determine who was right or wrong. Partisans at all points along the political spectrum were subject to the paradox we identified at the beginning of chapter 3: their worldview influenced what they saw as salient, and what they saw as salient influenced their worldview. That is, their symbolic world remained relatively closed. They understood events in such a way that certain aspects of context appeared salient, influencing, for instance, whether they took a broad or narrow view of the exchange between Mims and Trump, or whether they interpreted Trump's use of the word *animals* through the frame of history or security. The context they picked out then shaped how they understood what Trump meant. Each interpretive choice worked in this loop to confirm their pre-existing symbolic logic. For instance, those who interpreted Trump's comments through a security frame gave more weight to his mentions of violence, which led them to see MS-13 members as "animals" and reinforced the idea that the salient features of recent events involving U.S. Immigration and Customs Enforcement were the acts of violence (figure 31). Those who interpreted Trump's comments through a history frame, on the other hand, gave more weight to his history of nativist statements, which led them to see similar ideas now and reinforced the idea that the salient features of recent events related to his nativist appeals (figure 32). For this reason, any judgement we might make about who was right would fall along partisan lines because we, too, attribute more importance to certain aspects of context than others, an inescapably partisan choice.

39 Quoted in Qiu, "Context Behind Trump's 'Animals' Comment."

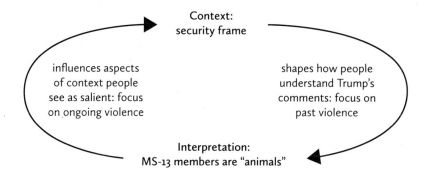

Figure 31. A feedback loop showing how people who focus on the violence mentioned by Trump also focus on violence in recent events.

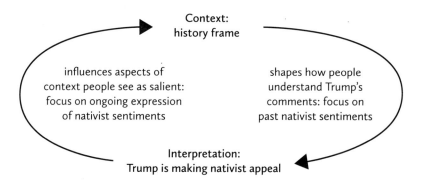

Figure 32. A feedback loop showing how people who focus on Trump's history of nativist comments also focus on his current expressions of nativist sentiments.

What matters instead is the strategy Trump used to implicate journalists in producing what he could point to as fake news. On May 18, he posted a tweet that made it look as though the *New York Times*, along with other outlets, had deliberately misrepresented his meaning:

Fake News Media had me calling Immigrants, or Illegal Immigrants, "Animals." Wrong! They were begrudgingly forced to withdraw their stories. I referred to MS 13 Gang Members as "Animals," a big difference—and so true. Fake News got it purposely wrong, as usual![40]

He was shifting blame and putting journalists on the defensive in such a way that the label *fake news* seemed all the more applicable.

At least one columnist at the *New York Times* agreed. Bret Stephens, a conservative columnist and frequent critic of Donald Trump, thought the coverage by his newspaper and others played into Trump's hands by supporting the story he wanted to tell about journalists. He pointed out retractions or clarifications made by the Associated Press and by Democratic politicians once the security frame became dominant (he did not acknowledge the plausibility of the history frame). "The president's apologists," he said, "can now point to a genuine instance of fake news—not merely factually mistaken, but wilfully misleading—in order to dismiss the great bulk of negative reporting that isn't fake."[41]

Stephens's column highlighted the impact of doubt on perspective. For Trump's supporters, the strategy of implicating journalists had the effect of casting them in a partisan light, undermining any claims they might make to neutrality and supporting (or appearing to support) Trump's claims that the news they produced was false. In this way, it strengthened associations with the security frame (figure 31) and weakened associations with the history frame (figure 32). Doubt became a tool for shifting the meaning of *fake news* so it was no longer a word used by journalists to describe made-up stories (as it was briefly after the 2016 election) but instead was a word used by people in positions of political power to describe stories they found troublesome.

40 From the Twitter account of @realDonaldTrump, May 18, 2018, https://twitter.com/realdonaldtrump/status/997429518867591170.

41 Bret Stephens, "Trump, MS-13, and Fake News."

Conclusion: Perspective Unmoored

Although we can't generalize from this one example, we can find others like it. In June 2018, for instance, journalist Liz Plank observed something similar in the controversy provoked by First Lady Melania Trump when she wore a jacket with the message "I REALLY DON'T CARE, DO U?" as she boarded a plane to visit an immigrant detention centre in Texas. Journalists criticized the message while spokespeople for the First Lady objected that it was only a jacket—something trivial and not worth the attention. Plank saw the jacket as bait that other journalists took, arguing that the decision to wear it

> creates a circus where . . . networks like Fox News can roll the clips and tweets from reporters being critical of [the First Lady's] choice of clothing to confirm to their viewers that the media cannot be trusted and that they don't focus on what the American people really care about.[42]

In other words, journalists acted out a script written by members of the Trump administration, which strengthened the idea that major news organizations were purveyors of fake news.

The proliferation of the term *fake news* has a broad range of implications, especially for the functioning of democracy in the United States and abroad, that others have addressed more effectively than I can here.[43] This analysis of the strategies Trump has used to shift the sense of the term does lead us to one useful conclusion, however. Carried to its logical extreme, the unmooring of perspective brought about by this shift encourages the growth of conspiracy theories grounded in a solipsism that follows a logic we saw in *Nineteen Eighty-Four*. People who believe these theories can explain away

---

42 Amira Rasool, "Journalist Liz Plank Believes the Media Was Baited by Melania Trump's Zara Jacket."

43 See, for instance, *New York Times* Editorial Board, "A Free Press Needs You" and "The True Damage of Trump's 'Fake News'"; and Michelle Goldberg, "The Autocrats' Playbook."

any evidence that would disprove them by arguing that it is really just manufactured by members of the conspiracy. Evidence produced by "fake news" outlets is no evidence at all because the source is not trustworthy.

The danger posed by this shift has increased as Trump and others have replaced the phrase *fake news* with the phrase *enemy of the people*. Trump himself has observed this change, as he wrote in a tweet in July 2018:

> Had a very good and interesting meeting at the White House with A. G. Sulzberger, Publisher of the New York Times. Spent much time talking about the vast amounts of Fake News being put out by the media & how that Fake News has morphed into phrase, "Enemy of the People." Sad![44]

Journalists worry that such rhetoric will lead to violence against them.[45]

Where does this analysis of the phrase *fake news*—along with that of Petr Pavlenskii and *Nineteen Eighty-Four* and "Encoding/Decoding"—leave us? We've explored the utopian and dystopian dimensions of cultural translation as a mode of substituting signs and changing people's perspectives. What are the implications for us as students and teachers living in the twenty-first century?

---

44 From the Twitter account of @realDonaldTrump, July 29, 2018, https://twitter.com/realDonaldTrump/status/1023546197129224192.

45 See, for example, Bret Stephens, "Trump Will Have Blood on His Hands"; and Scott Simon, "Opinion: Calling the Press the Enemy of the People Is a Menacing Move."

Conclusion
Jumping In

If you read enough scholarly books, you discover there's a formula for the concluding chapter. First, you summarize all the preceding chapters, making the links clear from one to the next. Second, you anticipate your critics' responses. What will they disagree with, and what will be the substance of their critique? (You then respond to them pre-emptively.) Third, you explain why any of this matters. You answer the eternal question: *So what? Who cares?*

I'm going to break from this formula, although I will address those concerns soon enough. Instead, I want to come back to a key idea in structuring this book, what in the introduction I called an epistemology of jumping in.[1] It brings together cultural translation, communication theory, and what they help us do.

To do that, I want to start with two stories.

Story one. When I was in late elementary school, I bought a television for my bedroom. I asked my parents if I could, and they—underestimating my resolve and willingness to delay gratification—said I could if I saved my own money. So for two years, I saved my allowance, rarely spending any of it, until I had $80. I bought a five-and-a-half inch black-and-white TV that got four fuzzy channels. I loved that thing, far more (I'm sure) than my parents would have liked.

---

1 Recall that epistemology is the branch of philosophy concerned with how we know what we know.

One day the on-off switch began to falter. It would turn on, but you'd have to hold it just right, or it'd flicker off again. At first I could live with it, but it got worse and worse. Soon I couldn't watch it at all. My dad said we could fix it. I asked him how, and he said he didn't know—we'd open it up and figure out it. I was pretty nervous—I saved up for two years to buy that thing, and he didn't even know how we'd fix it? He reassured me: once the case was open, we'd have the tools we needed to diagnose the problem and fix it.

What choice did I have?

So that's what we did. It turns out that for a split second, each time you turned it on the switch was carrying too much current. We put in a switch that could handle more current, and the TV worked for another fifteen years.

Story two. During the first week of my first year as an undergraduate at the University of North Dakota, I walked into the International Centre, where the study abroad programs were housed, and I knocked on the director's door. "Hi," I said, reaching out my hand. "I'm Kyle, and I want to study in France." (I get straight to the point when I've made up my mind.) "Okay," the director said. "Here are some programs. Where would you like to go?" I signed up to go to St. Étienne, a town about an hour from Lyon in southeastern France.

So it was that a year later, at age nineteen, I boarded an airplane bound for Paris, where I'd take a train to Caen for a three-week intensive language course, before finally heading to St. Étienne. I got to France and immediately made an alarming discovery (figure 33): my French classes in high school and university had not prepared me in any meaningful way to talk with French people. As eager a learner as I was, I wasn't prepared for how *fast* people talked, or for the fact that no one talked like they were in a textbook. (I mean, why would they?) Still, I had to eat, and for that, I had to talk. I also had to buy train tickets and ride buses and move into my room in the residence hall. I didn't have the tools I thought I had, but I clearly couldn't choose to do nothing. Hunger is a great motivator—I had to talk, even if I didn't know the words.

Figure 33. Me, arriving in St. Étienne, France, overconfident and about to discover just how little I know. Adapted from photograph by Nicolas Peyrard (2007, "Tramway de St. Étienne"), CC-BY 3.0. Source: Wikimedia Commons.

These two stories have something important in common: they're about acting even when I lacked the confidence to act. They're also about learning confidence through that process. In short, they're about the epistemology of jumping in—a way of coming to know the world by engaging in it and making mistakes.

What I mean is this. We base *every* decision on partial or incomplete information, not just the ones where the limits of what we know are clear, as in my two anecdotes. Still, even though we can't know everything about a situation, we're often faced with a choice. We can't choose to do nothing. (Even a choice not to act is a choice.) We learn to swim by jumping in, so to speak. In the process, we discover two things. First, we get a clearer sense of what we don't know. We find the gaps in our knowledge, the voids we need to fill. Second, we find that by acting, we begin to fill in those gaps.

Of course, jumping in always comes with a risk—we might be wrong, we might misread a situation, we might misjudge what we need to do. This is a common experience when we study abroad in a language that's not our own: we miss the unspoken cues that signal complicity or irony or humour. Everyone's laughing, and we don't know why. Here, too, we run a risk in not acting—we can be wrong in inaction just as much as in action. When we encounter a void, it can be difficult even to gauge which option is riskier. Do we laugh along, and risk perhaps hurting someone's feelings, or do we stay quiet, and make people feel awkward? Or do we smile feebly and hope someone will explain what's going on?

That's where this book is useful (or so I hope). Cultural translation and communication theory both provide tools for understanding how and where we jump in. Cultural translation—the idea that meaning is only relatively stable and that we can develop strategies for seeing the world differently (and persuading others to do the same)—is a general phenomenon, an everyday experience. Doing theory is a specific application: it consists in understanding how we use those strategies and in refining our understanding of them through observation and induction. Both are about making decisions based on incomplete information.

We'll spend the rest of this chapter exploring that link. We'll consider how an ungenerous critic might read my argument about cultural translation (but make no mistake—this critique is a constitutive component of my argument because without it my argument would be limp). We'll consider the role of communication theory as an application of cultural translation, and finally, we'll talk about why this matters. In short, it matters because, as an idea, cultural translation calls on us to examine our relations to others through the lens of ethics, and we cannot deny the humanness of the people who surround us.

Cultural Translation and the Epistemology of Jumping In

When scholars read, we do so with a well-honed skepticism. Our reflex is to doubt each claim, always making the same demand: *convince me.*

So as I write, I take on the role of a skeptical reader. And if I were reading this book, I'd find three main points of contention. First, my biggest critique would be that it lacks generalizable claims. It works from an odd collection of texts—I mean, really, who brings Claude Shannon, Warren Weaver, Stuart Hall, George Orwell, climate skeptics, Pussy Riot, Petr Pavlenskii, Aristotle, and Donald Trump together in the same book?—but with no statistics to tell us how we might apply the claims to other populations. How do we know any of this has changed anyone's mind, or is likely to in the future?

This observation is true, but it misses the point. I'd reply—in the academic jargon I likely share with such a reader—that this book is performative. Its structure is like that of chapter 1: it jumps into examples to encourage inductive reasoning. Consequently, my description in this concluding chapter is a metatheoretical account of that performative dimension (that is, it's theory about theory, and it describes how this book *works* to talk about what it *says*).

More simply, I'd say that the arguments I make are not generalizable in the way that social scientists might want. They do not involve random samples, and they have no statistical significance. In fact, they aren't falsifiable, meaning they do not have the capacity to be proven right or wrong. Instead, they rely on persuasion. They describe a logic they arrive at inductively, and they invite a response—they ask you to argue, refute, and improve. Moreover, *I* ask you to argue, refute, and improve. I ask *you*. (That's why I welcome a skeptical reading. I'd like to have a beer with my critic so we have time to talk. My reader brings a different set of tools that will help me refine these ideas. We'll refine them together.)

My second critique would also relate to the book's eclectic approach. It seems to lack order. It's spaghetti thrown against a wall to see what sticks.

To this I'd reply that jumping in is a way to act with necessarily incomplete knowledge. It's an epistemology of contingency and action, and it requires that we think on our toes. The eclectic selection of texts reflects that idea. Sometimes we need to improvise a tool when we discover a need. We need to dig, and for that, we look for a shovel. If we don't have one, we look at the tools we *do* have, we turn them around to get another view, and eventually we find one that will dig a hole (figure 34). Or we're in a foreign country, and we don't speak the language very well. There's an idea for which we don't know the word, but we don't have a dictionary at hand, so we improvise: we mime, we draw on a napkin, we use the words we do know to describe the one we don't. Our theoretical tools work the same way, as the parallax approach has shown. We pick them up, turn them around, and figure out which will do the trick. So eclectic, yes, but strategically so.

Figure 34. My workbench. It's a mess. Can you find a tool to dig with? Photograph by the author.

Finally, my third critique would be that the claims I've made about what we can know and how we can know it aren't applicable outside of the examples I give. In this case, I'd tend to agree. I'm making claims that apply to my classroom and my students, whom I ask to think about what we—together in the same space, at a regular time each week, subject as all people are to weather and traffic and jobs and grades—know and don't know. Naming what we know is straightforward enough: we know what it feels like to bump into the stubborn facts of the world.[2] Naming what we don't know is also straightforward: we don't know the stubborn facts of the world outside the mediation of our senses. Of course, a lot hinges on the key terms in those statements: *facts*, *world*, *senses*, words we come to understand in increasingly complex ways as we ask new questions to revise our old answers. Remember the three axioms I introduced in the introduction:

1. Theory is an attempt to explain our experience of the world.
2. If the explanation theory offers doesn't match our experience, it's bad theory.
   (2a. In the end, it's all bad theory.)
3. We must refine our explanation to replace bad theory with better theory.[3]

Even if we are concerned only with what we know in the classroom, this approach to theory has a built-in mechanism for refinement, and it will eventually pull us out into the wider world. It forces us to immerse ourselves in experience—in a word, to jump in.[4]

---

2 Or, if not the world, what we must pragmatically approach as "the world" if we want to avoid falling into the nihilistic solipsism of bad poststructuralism or paranoid internet echo chambers railing against all things "fake."

3 Note how these axioms evoke something different—a richer set of ideas, I hope— to you now than they did when you read them in the introduction.

4 Sam Rocha calls this approach "folk phenomenology," or the effort to relate our experience of the world, but without the specialized vocabulary we might develop if

Communication Theory and the Act of Jumping In

This built-in mechanism for refinement brings us back to an idea I introduced in the opening pages of the book, that of theory as *technē*, or a craft we learn by practicing, like music or art. It's a set of skills, a way of training ourselves to be aware of our perception and experience of the world—and, more to the point, of communication. The best way to develop these skills is by using them—to jump into theory, that foreign language (as I also wrote in the opening pages), and learn them as we go.

To put that idea into practice, I structured the book to follow the three axioms. After the introduction, chapter 1 offered an explanation of one aspect of communication. To use a sign, it argued, is to transform and translate it. Words accumulate meaning as people respond to each other and take their respective responses into account. Even from one use to the next, a word doesn't evoke exactly the same thing—a gap opens up, even if it's slight. That idea led me to assert that this process of transformation and translation "opens up a space for a politics of invention," as I wrote, "where we can rethink our relation to cultural others so that people we once feared can find their place in the communities we claim as our own."

That was axiom 1 (theory as explanation). Chapters 2 to 4 tested that explanation. Of course, I mean "tested" in a different way than a social scientist. "Testing" in the humanities-oriented sense, as I use it here, means using stories or art we find compelling to help think through the implications of an argument. Thus chapter 2 reveals ways this translation can help us know the world in new ways, but also how it can loosen our grip on what we think we know. Chapter 3 helps us develop tools to persuade each other and ground our experience, while chapter 4 shows how those tools, too, can cut both ways.

---

studied phenomenology in a formal sense. See Rocha, *Folk Phenomenology: Education, Study, and the Human Person.*

That was axiom 2 (theory's *potential* fallibility) and its corollary, 2a (its *certain* fallibility). Chapter 1 argued that cultural translation can make society more inclusive, but it overlooked the ways it can also lead to oppression and exclusion. Part of the explanation did not match our experience of the world, where oppression remains a very real phenomenon, so we had to revise it. Hence chapter 2, whose purpose was to improve the initial explanation by identifying its limits. Chapters 3 and 4 followed the same pattern. Chapter 3 proposed tools for changing people's minds, based on the explanation developed in the chapters before it. But it, too, fell short, failing to account for the negative potential of those tools. Hence chapter 4, whose purpose— again—was to improve the explanation by identifying its limits.

Where does that leave us? We arrive at axiom 3, concerned with theory's refinement. The preceding chapters were the back-and-forth exchange (between me and my students and my imagined readers) that helped us arrive at a clearer understanding of cultural trans- lation and communication: we've replaced faulty explanations with better explanations. That effort is the impetus for the idea of jumping in, which this conclusion has developed. It's an approach that forces us to recognize that we can't anticipate everything we'll encounter. We'll have to improvise, based on the situations we encounter. That recognition is the key refinement to the theories proposed in chapters 1 to 4, a way to extend or even surpass the tool of the parallax view.

But here's where things get trippy. My three axioms also apply to metatheory, or explanations about what theory is. They, too, can be tested and found lacking. What happens if we take a step back and treat my axioms themselves as an explanation of our experience of the world? In other words (there's that phrase again!), what hap- pens if we rewrite the axioms by substituting specific observations for the general ones I've now repeated across multiple chapters? The axioms become:

1. We operate in the world by explaining it, testing our explanations, and refining them as necessary.
2. If we do not operate this way, our metatheory falls short. (2a. In the end, all metatheory falls short.)
3. We must refine our explanation by accounting for those things our initial formulation left out.

Where does that formulation fall short? In the analysis in chapters 1 to 4, my focus was on developing concepts, and the explanations I put forward and critiqued served that purpose. I wanted to show how cultural translation has more than one valence: it can include or exclude, provide perspective or remove it. But we are more than merely cerebral creatures, and we deal with more than just concepts. The assertion that we can generalize my approach to talk about how we come to know the broader world simplifies our interactions with other people (who, of course, are part of that broader world). It misses a key aspect of our lives, namely the value we assign to our actions.

How do we refine this assertion? How do we account for the dimensions of experience that it overlooks? The answer lies in an idea that has been present throughout the book but has remained, until now, more or less latent. It is the idea of ethics.

Conclusion: Cultural Translation and the Call to Ethics

Communication scholar John Durham Peters reminds us of something fundamental and important to remember here: communication always involves two people.[5] As a result, "communication theory becomes consubstantial with ethics, political philosophy, and social theory in its concern for relations between self and other, self and self, and closeness and distance in social organizations."[6] Whenever

5 Even when I talk to myself, I imagine myself as if I were someone else, as if I stepped out of my body and am talking to someone else.

6 John Durham Peters, *Speaking into the Air: A History of the Idea of Communication*, 10.

there are two people in relation to each other, they have to figure out how to act, and one dimension of that process is that of ethics.

The same is true of cultural translation. In its positive valence—when we use it to make society more inclusive—it implies an ethical stance and an openness toward others. If we were not open to others, we wouldn't engage with them, instead trying simply to impose our will. (Of course, some people *do* take that approach. They're not open to others, and they refuse to engage with them.) Cultural translation requires us to strike a balance between finding things in common and respecting difference. It can bring others closer but in a way that they maintain their sense of self. We have to be careful not to say "Oh, you're just like me!" if doing so causes us to miss important ways people are different. Such an attitude might make us feel like we're being inclusive, but if it denies people an essential part of themselves, then that feeling is tragically misleading. We can't know others in any definitive way, any more than we can know the world in a definitive way. Instead, we jump into a relation with them and fill in the gaps as we go.

This task is not easy, especially when we are mindful of an observation I made in the introductory chapter: people—even those on opposite sides of a conflict—tend to see themselves as the good guys. We all think we're the scrappy rebels from *Star Wars*, and our adversaries belong to the villainous Empire. So what is the difference between groups who use cultural translation to encourage inclusion and those who use it to oppress? It is their humility, in the form of openness to the possibility they might be wrong. The Party in *Nineteen Eighty-Four*, for instance, makes the a priori assumption that it is right, and it uses force to impose its will. I suspect that the people who use the phrase "fake news" to enclose others in a solipsistic, perspectiveless world do something similar. On the other hand, the judge in Brecht's poem (about the immigrant who answers "1492" to every question the judge asks) is open to the idea that he might be wrong, or the that system he represents might be wrong. His invention is not reliant on force. Similarly, Petr Pavlenskii does not rely on force. Instead, he invites people to see the world as he does, relying on the strategy of showing them how they are implicated in the system he wants to change.

How do we avoid imposing our will? Over the course of this book, I have described three dimensions of cultural translation, the first two of which are power and meaning. They influence each other: power shapes the way people talk about things, and thus the meaning they attribute to them (or the meaning those things evoke). Power can derive from social structure or from force, and its roots are in the history of interactions and resulting relations between people, in small groups and large. At the same time, meaning influences power. Its roots are related, as they, too, are in the history of interactions between people.

The third dimension is that of creation or invention, which can be playful or serious or both, a way—at least potentially—to turn meaning against power. Everything hinges on this third dimension. Everything hinges on invention. If cultural translation has anything to teach us about communication, it is this: we can open up space for others when we recognize that we ourselves might be wrong. In doing so, we address one of the critiques raised in the introductory chapter: we have taken the necessary first step for finding common ground for negotiating the meaning we make of the world. This recognition leads to a specific strategy for invention, one that can be summed up quite simply: listen first, speak second. Ask first, tell second. In this way, we arrive at an unexpected answer to the question that opens this book.

How do we change people's minds? By opening ourselves to the possibility that they might change our minds, too.

Notes on Teaching

There are at least three approaches to teaching communication theory. Perhaps the most common is to organize a course around different subfields or traditions. Robert Craig and Heidi Muller provide the best model of this approach in *Theorizing Communication*, a book I have often used, but with certain reservations. The subfield-based approach is paradoxical: what starts out as a descriptive model *of* theory ends up becoming a prescriptive model *for* theory, to borrow a distinction from James Carey.[1] Less abstractly, Craig and Muller begin by describing communication theory as its practitioners have developed it. They argue that the subfields they identify are those that theorists themselves have created. But by dividing communication into subfields, they simultaneously create a set of templates for how to do theoretical inquiry, which professors reproduce when they organize a class along subfield lines. Professors run the risk of taking their object of study—theory—for granted, when instead they should be asking students to approach it critically. For that reason I tell my students, if you're going to take a subfield-oriented approach, their book is the best you'll find, but you need to examine their premise with a healthy skepticism.

A second approach is historical, exemplified by John Durham Peters's *Speaking into the Air* or Armand Mattelart's *L'invention de*

---

1 James Carey, "A Cultural Approach to Communication," 25.

la communication. It consists in reading what people have had to say about communication, starting perhaps with Plato's *Gorgias* or *Phaedrus*, followed by Aristotle's *Rhetoric*, then working through the present day. The problem with this approach, however, is that it requires a familiarity with communication theory from the outset, something third-year undergraduates enrolled in a survey course typically don't have. I have taken this approach at the graduate level, however.

Finally, the third approach is the one I adopt here. It consists in asking what we mean by the word *theory* and the competing ideas it evokes. My goal is to equip students to read the types of arguments they would encounter in a class that adopted either of the other two approaches. I want them to see that theorists respond to and argue with each other about the nature of the phenomena they set themselves the task of describing.

I structure the course as a reconstructed conversation about a series of questions, some abstract, some more concrete, that communication theorists have asked. Each chapter of *The Art of Communication in a Polarized World* makes use of ideas others have developed, and I give students essays by those people first. In that way, the book chapter is a turn taken in this conversation, and the questions I ask prompt students to take their turn, too.

Engaging Students in the Conversation About Theory

I have adopted two strategies for engaging students in the conversation about theory. First, at the end of each lesson, I ask open-ended questions to provoke discussion. The questions change depending on the students' interests and proclivity for talking, but they usually focus attention on a concrete object.[2] Their purpose is twofold. For

---

2 To discuss solipsism, for instance, the *Black Mirror* episode "San Junipero" has prompted rather heated discussions about the nature of reality and our ability to know it through our senses.

one thing, they ground students' reading in the here-and-now, not in some abstract world where academic ideas often seem to live. For another, they bridge the gap between chapters by priming students to think about the themes in the chapter that follows. In this way, if I'm successful, the questions draw students into the conversation I've manufactured and give them a way of jumping into the practice of theory.

The second strategy has been to incorporate creative works, such as novels, television, and poetry. These works serve three purposes. First, they demonstrate different ways to ask questions about communication (and translation). I want to claim a place for the humanities in conversations about communication theory, which has its roots in philosophy, as the references to Plato and Aristotle make clear. I emphasize communication's long history in humanistic thought, not to the exclusion of the social sciences, but instead as their conceptual foundation.[3] Second, creative works invite students to explore the world from other perspectives. As Kwame Anthony Appiah writes, "Conversations across boundaries of identity—whether national, religious, or something else—begin with the sort of imaginative engagement you get when you read a novel or watch a movie or attend to a work of art that speaks from some place other than your own."[4] Finally, they're fun. They engage students. A cynic might accuse me of pandering, but I'm not. We need to take students seriously. Consequently, we need to recognize the importance of speaking to them about things that matter to them. Not every creative work will appeal to every student, to be sure, but I try to incorporate a wide enough variety that students will find something that speaks to them. Theory, I insist, is meaningful only if it explains things that matter.

3 Although social scientists might not recognize the humanistic roots of their work, without the humanities, it could not exist. Methods textbooks, for instance, are built on a foundation of epistemology and rhetoric, manifest (among other places) in their discussions of what claims can be made and supported or how they might be most persuasively presented.

4 Kwame Anthony Appiah, *Cosmopolitanism: Ethics in a World of Strangers*, 85.

Syllabus

I am including below the essentials of the syllabus I have followed when using *The Art of Communication in a Polarized World* to teach my third-year undergraduate course. The syllabus evolves each semester and will no doubt change the next time I teach the course.

ADVANCED THEORIES IN COMMUNICATION

Rationale and Objectives

Communication theory is nothing more than an attempt to explain what communication is. Sometimes we ask broadly about exchange, transmission, and ritual. Sometimes we ask narrowly about how what we share in specific situations affects the people we share it with. But in all cases, that explanation is our goal.

In this course, we will explore communication theory by reading answers people have given to a series of questions that start broadly: What is theory? What is communication? How does speech shape thought? Then the questions narrow down: How do we change people's minds? How can we be confident in what we read? The readings recreate a conversation of sorts, as people respond to each other and develop their ideas. This conversation leads to our final question, namely, What does it mean to do theory? How do *we* participate in this conversation?

By the end of the course, you should be able to:

- identify and explain conflicting ways people have answered questions about communication;
- find and use evidence to answer questions about communication; and
- investigate communication in new ways by generating new questions.

Required Reading

The Art of Communication in a Polarized World
Individual articles as listed in the reading schedule[5]

Reading Schedule

Week 1   Introduction: What are we doing here?
Readings*: Art of Communication*, Preface; Korb, "The
Soul-Crushing Student Essay"

Week 2   What is theory? (part 1)
Readings: Craig, "Communication Theory as a Field";
Carey, "A Cultural Approach to Communication"

Week 3   What is theory? (part 2)
Reading: *Art of Communication*, Introduction

Week 4   What is communication? (part 1)
Readings: Weaver, "The Mathematics of Communication"; Hall, "Encoding/Decoding"

Week 5   What is communication? (part 2)
Readings: Merrell, "Charles Sanders Peirce's Concept of
the Sign"; *Art of Communication*, Chapter 1

Week 6   How does speech shape thought? (part 1)
Readings: Sapir, "The Status of Linguistics as a Science";
Bakhtin, "The Problem of Speech Genres" (excerpt)

Week 7   How does speech shape thought? (part 2)
Readings: Nastasia and Rakow, "What Is Theory?"; *Art of
Communication*, Chapter 2

Week 8   How do we change people's minds? (part 1)
Readings: Aristotle, *Rhetoric* (excerpt); Aristotle, *The Art
of Poetry* (excerpt)

---

5 Full citations for the readings are in the bibliography.

Week 9 How do we change people's minds? (part 2)
Reading: *Art of Communication*, Chapter 3

Week 10 How can we be confident in what we read? (part 1)
Readings: Tuchman, "Objectivity as a Strategic Ritual";
Gauthier, "In Defence of a Supposedly Outdated Notion"

Week 11 How can we be confident in what we read? (part 2)
Reading: *Art of Communication*, Chapter 4

Week 12 Conclusion: How do we do theory?
Reading: *Art of Communication*, Conclusion

Bibliography

Albeck-Ripka, Livia. "How Six Americans Changed Their Minds About Global Warming." *New York Times*, February 21, 2018. https://nyti.ms/2BEZovQ.

Appiah, Kwame Anthony. *Cosmopolitanism: Ethics in a World of Strangers*. New York: Norton, 2006.

Aristotle. *On the Art of Poetry*. Translated by Ingram Bywater. Oxford: Clarendon Press, 1920. https://archive.org/details/aristotleonartoooaris.

———. *Rhetoric*. Translated by W. Rhys Roberts. Cambridge, MA: MIT Internet Classics Archive, 1994. http://classics.mit.edu/Aristotle/rhetoric.html.

———. *Topics*. Translated by W. A. Pickard-Cambridge. Cambridge, MA: MIT Internet Classics Archive, 1994. http://classics.mit.edu/Aristotle/topics.html.

Astore, William J. "Can You Spot the American Military in Your Favorite Sci-Fi Film? Hint: We're Always the Bad Guys." *The Nation*, July 12, 2016. https://www.thenation.com/article/can-you-spot-the-american-military-in-your-favorite-sci-fi-film/.

Bakhtin, Mikhail. "The Problem of Speech Genres." Translated by Vern W. McGee. In *The Lyric Theory Reader: A Critical Anthology*, edited by Virginia Jackson and Yopie Prins, 224–34. Baltimore: Johns Hopkins University Press, 2014.

———. *Speech Genres and Other Late Essays*. Translated by Vern W. McGee. Austin: University of Texas Press, 1986.

Bassnett, Susan. "The Translation Turn in Cultural Studies." In *Constructing Cultures: Essays on Literary Translation*, edited by Susan Bassnett and André Lefevere, 123–40. Philadelphia: Multilingual Matters, 1998.

Baumgartner, Jody, and Jonathan S. Morris. "The *Daily Show* Effect: Candidate Evaluations, Efficacy, and American Youth." *American Politics Research* 34, no. 3 (2006): 341–67. https://dx.doi.org/10.1177/1532673X05280074.

Berman, Antoine. "Translation and the Trials of the Foreign." Translated by Lawrence Venuti. In *The Translation Studies Reader*, edited by Lawrence Venuti, 284–97. New York: Routledge, 2000.

Bhabha, Homi K. *The Location of Culture*. New York: Routledge, 1994.

Bielsa, Esperança, and Susan Bassnett. *Translation in Global News*. New York: Routledge, 2009.

Bodin, Per-Arne. "Petr Pevlenskii and His Actions." In Jonson and Erofeev, *Russia—Art Resistance and the Conservative-Authoritarian Zeitgeist*, 271–78.

Bourdieu, Pierre. *On Television*. Translated by Priscilla Parkhurst Ferguson. New York: New Press, 1996.

Bryzgel, Amy. "Chopped Earlobes and the Long History of Political Shock Art in Russia." *The Conversation*, December 15, 2014. https://theconversation.com/chopped-earlobes-and-the-long-history-of-political-shock-art-in-russia-35233.

Buden, Boris, and Stefan Nowotny. "Cultural Translation: An Introduction to the Problem." *Translation Studies* 2, no. 2 (2009): 196–208. https://dx.doi.org/10.1080/14781700902937730.

Caraher, Wiliam, Kostis Kourelis, and Andrew Reinhard, eds. *Punk Archaeology*. Grand Forks, ND: Digital Press at the University of North Dakota, 2014. https://thedigitalpress.org/portfolio/punk-archaeology/.

Carey, James. "A Cultural Approach to Communication." In *Communication as Culture: Essays on Media and Society*, rev. ed., 11–28. New York: Routledge, 2009.

———. "Technology and Ideology: The Case of the Telegraph." In *Communication as Culture: Essays on Media and Society*, rev. ed., 155–77. New York: Routledge, 2009.

Carpenter, Amanda. *Gaslighting America: Why We Love It When Trump Lies to Us*. New York: Broadside, 2018.

Chalaby, Jean. "Journalism as an Anglo-American Invention: A Comparison of the Development of French and Anglo-American Journalism, 1830s–1920s." *European Journal of Communication* 11, no. 3 (1996): 303–26.

Chen, Adrian. "The Agency." *New York Times Magazine*, June 2, 2015. https://www.nytimes.com/2015/06/07/magazine/the-agency.html.

Clifford, James, and George E. Marcus, eds. *Writing Culture: The Poetics and Politics of Ethnography*. Berkeley: University of California Press, 1986.

Conway, Kyle. "Communication Is Translation, or, How to Mind the Gap." *Palabra Clave* 20, no. 3 (2017): 622–44. https://dx.doi.org/10.5294/pacla.2017.20.3.2.

————. "A Conceptual and Empirical Approach to Cultural Translation." *Translation Studies* 5, no. 3 (2012): 264–79. https://dx.doi.org/10.1080/1478 1700.2012.701938.

————. "Cultural Translation, Global Television Studies, and the Circulation of Telenovelas in the United States." *International Journal of Cultural Studies* 15 (2012): 583–98. https://dx.doi.org/10.1177/1367877911422291.

————. "Cultural Translation." In *Routledge Encyclopedia of Translation Studies*, 3rd ed., edited by Mona Baker and Gabriela Saldanha, 129–33. London: Routledge, 2020.

————. "Cultural Translation: Two Modes." *TTR: Traduction, Terminologie, Rédaction* 26, no. 1 (2013): 15–36. https://dx.doi.org/10.7202/1036948ar.

————. "Encoding/Decoding as Translation." *International Journal of Communication* 11 (2017): 710–27. https://ijoc.org/index.php/ijoc/article/ view/5922.

————. Little Mosque on the Prairie *and the Paradoxes of Cultural Translation*. Toronto: University of Toronto Press, 2017.

————. "Modern Hospitality." *North Dakota Quarterly* 84, nos. 1–2 (2017): 185–94. https://ndquarterly.org/2017/08/24/kyle-conway-modern-hospitality/.

Craig, Robert T. "Communication Theory as a Field." *Communication Theory* 9, no. 2 (1999): 119–61. https://doi.org/10.1111/j.1468-2885.1999.tb00355.x.

Craig, Robert T., and Heidi L. Muller, eds. *Theorizing Communication: Readings Across Traditions*. Thousand Oaks, CA: Sage, 2007.

Culler, Jonathan. *Literary Theory: A Very Short Introduction*. New York: Oxford University Press, 1997.

Dalton, Dan. "14 Perfect French Words and Phrases We Need in English." *BuzzFeed*, June 22, 2015. https://www.buzzfeed.com/danieldalton/ exquisite-pain.

Davis, Julie Hirschfeld. "Trump Calls Some Unauthorized Immigrants 'Animals' in Rant." *New York Times*, May 16, 2018. https://www.nytimes. com/2018/05/16/us/politics/trump-undocumented-immigrants-animals. html.

Davis, Julie Hirschfeld, and Niraj Chokshi. "Trump Defends 'Animals' Remark, Saying It Referred to MS-13 Gang Members." *New York Times*, May 17, 2018. https://www.nytimes.com/2018/05/17/us/trump-animals-ms-13-gangs.html.

Deeg, Kathryn S., Erik Lyon, Anthony Leiserowitz, Edward Maibach, John Kotcher, and Jennifer Marlon. "Who Is Changing Their Mind About Global

Warming and Why?" Climate Note, Yale Program on Climate Change
Communication. January 9, 2019. https://climatecommunication.yale.edu/
publications/who-is-changing-their-mind-about-global-warming-and-why/.

Demont-Heinrich, Christof. Review of *Translation in Global News*, by
Esperança Bielsa and Susan Bassnett. *Journal of Sociolinguistics* 15, no. 3
(2011): 402–5. https://dx.doi.org/10.1111/j.1467-9841.2011.00492.x.

Derakhshan, Hossein, and Claire Wardle. "Information Disorder: Definitions."
Paper prepared for "Understanding and Addressing the Disinformation
Ecosystem," a workshop held at the Annenberg School for Communication,
University of Pennsylvania, Philadelphia, December 15–16, 2017. In
Understanding and Addressing the Disinformation Ecosystem, 5–12. https://
firstdraftnews.org/wp-content/uploads/2018/03/The-Disinformation-
Ecosystem-20180207-v4.pdf.

De Winne, Lena [*Лена Де Винне*]. *"Допрос Петра Павленского. Пьеса в трех
действиях* [The Interrogation of Petr Pavlenskii: A Play in Three Acts]."
Сноб, July 29, 2014. https://snob.ru/selected/entry/77648.

Dole, Janice A., and Gale M. Sinatra. "Reconceptualizing Change in the
Cognitive Construction of Knowledge." *Educational Psychologist* 33, nos. 2–3
(1998): 109–28.

du Gay, Paul, Stuart Hall, Linda Janes, Hugh Mackay, and Keith Negus. *Doing
Cultural Studies: The Story of the Sony Walkman*. Thousand Oaks, CA: Sage,
1997.

During, Simon. "More Orwell." *Public Books*, May 31, 2017. http://www.
publicbooks.org/more-orwell/.

Entman, Robert M. "Framing: Toward Clarification of a Fractured
Paradigm." *Journal of Communication* 43, no. 3 (1993): 51–58. https://doi.
org/10.1111/j.1460-2466.1993.tb01304.x.

Eshun, Ekow, Maryam Omidi, Jamie Rann, and Igor Zinatulin. "The Naked
Truth: The Art World Reacts to Pyotr Pavlensky's Red Square Protest."
Calvert Journal, November 14, 2013. http://www.calvertjournal.com/
articles/show/1768/pyotr-pavlensky-russian-artist-nails-red-square.

Fletcher, Richard, and Rasmus Kleis Nielsen. "People Don't Trust News
Media—and This Is Key to the Global Misinformation Debate." Paper
prepared for "Understanding and Addressing the Disinformation
Ecosystem," a workshop held at the Annenberg School for Communication,
University of Pennsylvania, Philadelphia, December 15–16, 2017. In
Understanding and Addressing the Disinformation Ecosystem, 13–17. https://

firstdraftnews.org/wp-content/uploads/2018/03/The-Disinformation-Ecosystem-20180207-v4.pdf.

Franklin, Ruth. "Tracy K. Smith, America's Poet Laureate, Is a Woman with a Mission." *New York Times Magazine*, April 10, 2018. https://nyti. ms/2HnHpZT.

Frimer, Jeremy A., Linda J. Skitka, and Matt Motyl. "Liberals and Conservatives Are Similarly Motivated to Avoid Exposure to One Another's Opinions." *Journal of Experimental Social Psychology* 72 (2017): 1–12. https:// doi.org/10.1016/j.jesp.2017.04.003.

Gauthier, Gilles. "In Defence of a Supposedly Outdated Notion: The Range of Application of Journalistic Objectivity." Translated by Carole Small. *Canadian Journal of Communication* 18, no. 4 (1993). https://cjc-online.ca/ index.php/journal/article/view/778/684.

Gibson, Walker. "Truisms Are True: Orwell's View of Language." In Lutz, *Beyond Nineteen Eighty-Four*, 11–16.

Goffman, Erving. *Frame Analysis: An Essay on the Organization of Experience.* Cambridge, MA: Harvard University Press, 1974.

Goldberg, Michelle. "The Autocrats' Playbook." *New York Times*, April 2, 2018. https://www.nytimes.com/2018/04/02/opinion/trump-autocrat-playbook. html.

Greenberg, Jon, Louis Jacobson, and Manuela Tobias. "Fact-Checking Donald Trump's Fake News Awards." *Politifact*, January 18, 2018. https://www. politifact.com/truth-o-meter/article/2018/jan/18/fact-checking-donald-trumps-fake-news-awards/.

Guldin, Rainer. "From Transportation to Transformation: On the Use of the Metaphor of Translation Within Media and Communication Theory." *Global Media Journal—Canadian Edition* 5, no. 1 (2012): 39–52. http://gmj-canadianedition.ca//wp-content/uploads/2018/11/v5i1_guldin.pdf.

Hall, Stuart. "Encoding and Decoding in the Television Discourse." Paper prepared for the Council of Europe Colloquy "Training in the Critical Reading of Televisual Language" held at the University of Leicester, September 1973. CCCS Stencilled Occasional Papers no. 7 (1973). https:// www.birmingham.ac.uk/Documents/college-artslaw/history/cccs/ stencilled-occasional-papers/1to8and11to24and38to48/SOP07.pdf.

———. "Cultural Studies: Two Paradigms." *Media, Culture and Society* 2 (1980): 57–72. https://dx.doi.org/10.1177/016344378000200106.

———. "Encoding/Decoding." In *Culture, Media, Language*, edited by Stuart Hall, Dorothy Hobson, Andrew Lowe, and Paul Willis, 128–38. London: Hutchinson, 1980.

Hall, Stuart, ed. *Representation: Cultural Representations and Signifying Practices*. Thousand Oaks, CA: Sage, 1997.

Hodgson, Naomi, Joris Vlieghe, and Piotr Zamojski. *Manifesto for a Post-critical Pedagogy*. Brooklyn, NY: Punctum Books, 2017. https://punctumbooks.com/titles/manifesto-for-a-post-critical-pedagogy/.

Horkheimer, Max, and Theodor W. Adorno. "The Culture Industry: Enlightenment as Mass Deception." 1944. In *Dialectic of Enlightenment*, translated by John Cumming, 120–67. London: Verso, 1997. Abridged version, Marxists Internet Archive, https://www.marxists.org/reference/archive/adorno/1944/culture-industry.htm.

Howe, Irving, ed. *Orwell's Nineteen Eighty-Four: Text, Sources, Criticism*. 2nd ed. New York: Harcourt Brace Jovanovich, 1982.

Husserl, Edmund. *The Crisis of the European Sciences and Transcendental Phenomenology: An Introduction to Phenomenological Philosophy*. Translated by David Carr. Evanston, IL: Northwestern University Press, 1970.

Jones, Jeffrey P. *Entertaining Politics: Satiric Television and Political Engagement*. 2nd ed. Lanham, MD: Rowman and Littlefield, 2010.

Jonson, Lena, and Andrei Erofeev, eds. *Russia—Art Resistance and the Conservative-Authoritarian Zeitgeist*. New York: Routledge, 2017.

Kakutani, Michiko. "Why '1984' Is a 2017 Must-Read." *New York Times*, January 26, 2017. https://www.nytimes.com/2017/01/26/books/why-1984-is-a-2017-must-read.html.

Keith, Tamara. "President Trump's Description of What's 'Fake' Is Expanding." National Public Radio, September 2, 2018. https://www.npr.org/2018/09/02/643761979/president-trumps-description-of-whats-fake-is-expanding.

Kershner, Irvin, dir. *The Empire Strikes Back*. Los Angeles: 20th Century Fox.

Kim, Sujeong. "Rereading David Morley's *The 'Nationwide' Audience*." *Cultural Studies* 18, no. 1 (2004): 84–108. https://dx.doi.org/10.1080/0950238042000181629.

Korb, Scott. "The Soul-Crushing Student Essay." *New York Times*, April 21, 2018. https://www.nytimes.com/2018/04/21/opinion/the-soul-crushing-student-essay.html.

Lazer, David M. J., Matthew A. Baum, Yochai Benkler, Adam J. Berinsky, Kelly M. Greenhill, Filippo Menezer, Miriam J. Metzger, Brendan Nyhan, Gordon

Pennycook, David Rothschild, Michael Schudson, Steven A. Sloman, Cass R. Sunstein, Emily A. Thorson, Duncan J. Watts, and Jonathan L. Zittrain. "The Science of Fake News." *Science* 359 (2018): 1094–96. https://science. sciencemag.org/content/359/6380/1094.

Lienhardt, Godfrey. "Modes of Thought." In *The Institutions of Primitive Society: A Series of Broadcast Talks*, by E. E. Evans-Pritchard, Raymond Firth, E. R. Leach, J. G. Peristiany, John Layard, Max Gluckman, Meyer Fortes, and Godfrey Lienhardt. Oxford: Basil Blackwell, 1954. https:// archive.org/details/institutionsofpro33235mbp.

Liszka, James Jakób. *A General Introduction to the Semeiotic of Charles Sanders Peirce*. Bloomington: Indiana University Press, 1996.

Longinovic, Tomislav Z. "Fearful Asymmetries: A Manifesto of Cultural Translation." *Journal of the Midwest Modern Language Association* 35, no. 2 (2002): 5–12. https://dx.doi.org/10.2307/1315162.

Lucas, George, dir. *Star Wars*. Los Angeles: 20th Century Fox, 1977.

Lutz, William. *Beyond Nineteen Eighty-Four: Doublespeak in a Post-Orwellian Age*. Urbana, IL: National Council of Teachers of English, 1989. https://files. eric.ed.gov/fulltext/ED311451.pdf.

——. "Notes Toward a Definition of Doublespeak." In Lutz, *Beyond Nineteen Eighty-Four: Doublespeak in a Post-Orwellian Age*, 1–10.

Maitland, Sarah. *What Is Cultural Translation?* London: Bloomsbury, 2017.

Marx, Karl. *Grundrisse: Foundations of the Critique of Political Economy*. 1857– 58. Translated by Martin Nicolaus. London: Penguin Books, 1973. Marxists Internet Archive, https://www.marxists.org/archive/marx/works/1857/ grundrisse/.

——. "Theses on Feuerbach." 1845. Translated by W. Lough. Moscow: Progress Publishers, 1969. Marxists Internet Archive, https://www. marxists.org/archive/marx/works/1845/theses/theses.htm.

Mattelart, Armand. *L'invention de la communication*. Paris: Découverte, 1994.

——. *The Invention of Communication*. Translated by Susan Emanuel. Minneapolis: University of Minnesota Press, 1996.

Mercieca, Jennifer. "There's an Insidious Strategy Behind Donald Trump's Retweets." *The Conversation*, March 8, 2016. https://theconversation.com/ theres-an-insidious-strategy-behind-donald-trumps-retweets-55615.

Merrell, Floyd. "Charles Sanders Peirce's Concept of the Sign." In *The Routledge Companion to Semiotics and Linguistics*, edited by Paul Cobley, 28–39. New York: Routledge, 2001.

Michel, Jean-Baptiste, Yuan Kui Shen, Aviva Presser Aiden, Adrian Veres, Matthew K. Gray, William Brockman, The Google Books Team, Joseph P. Pickett, Dale Hoiberg, Dan Clancy, Peter Norvig, Jon Orwant, Steven Pinker, Martin A. Nowak, and Erez Lieberman Aiden. "Quantitative Analysis of Culture Using Millions of Digitized Books." *Science* 331, no. 6014 (2011): 176–82. https://dx.doi.org/10.1126/science.1199644.

Mitchell, Amy, Jeffrey Gottfried, Michael Barthel, and Elisa Shearer. *The Modern News Consumer: News Attitudes and Practices in the Digital Era.* Washington, DC: Pew Research Center, July 7, 2016. https://www.issuelab. org/resources/24985/24985.pdf.

Moran, Albert. *New Flows in Global TV.* Chicago: Intellect, 2009.

Morley, David. *The "Nationwide" Audience: Structure and Decoding.* London: British Film Institute, 1980.

Nastasia, Diana Iulia, and Lana F. Rakow. "What Is Theory? Puzzles and Maps as Metaphors in Communication Theory." *tripleC: Communication, Capitalism and Critique* 8, no. 1 (2010): 1–17. https://triple-c.at/index.php/ tripleC/article/view/137.

Nechepurenko, Ivan. "How Russia's 'Most Controversial Artist' Persuaded His Interrogator to Change Sides." *The Guardian*, July 28, 2015. https://www. theguardian.com/world/2015/jul/28/petr-pavlensky-artist-scrotum-red- square-interrogator.

New York Times Editorial Board. "The Cruelty of Breaking Up Immigrant Families." *New York Times*, May 17, 2018. https://www.nytimes. com/2018/05/17/opinion/trump-immigrant-families-separation- deportation.html.

———. "A Free Press Needs You." *New York Times*, August 15, 2018. https:// www.nytimes.com/interactive/2018/08/15/opinion/editorials/free-press- local-journalism-news-donald-trump.html.

———. "The True Damage of Trump's 'Fake News.'" *New York Times*, April 4, 2018. https://www.nytimes.com/2018/04/04/opinion/trump-washington- post-amazon.html.

Nordgaard, Ingrid. "Documenting/Performing the Vulnerable Body: Pain and Agency in Works by Boris Mikhailov and Petr Pavlensky." *Contemporaneity: Historical Presence in Visual Culture* 5, no. 1 (2016): 85–107. https://dx.doi. org/10.5195/contemp.2016.184.

Orwell, George. *Nineteen Eighty-Four.* In Howe, *Orwell's* Nineteen Eighty- Four, 3–205.

————. "Politics and the English Language." In Howe, *Orwell's* Nineteen Eighty-Four, 248–59.

Pavlenskii, Petr, and Pavel Yasman. "A Dialogue About Art." In Jonson and Erofeev, *Russia—Art Resistance and the Conservative-Authoritarian Zeitgeist*, 279–91.

Peirce, Charles. *The Philosophy of Peirce: Selected Writings*. Edited by Justus Buchler. London: Routledge and Kegan, 1940.

Peters, John Durham. *Speaking into the Air: A History of the Idea of Communication*. Chicago: University of Chicago Press, 1999.

Plato. *Gorgias*. Translated by Benjamin Jowett. Cambridge, MA: MIT Internet Classics Archive, 1994. http://classics.mit.edu/Plato/gorgias.html.

————. *Phaedrus*. Translated by Benjamin Jowett. Cambridge, MA: MIT Internet Classics Archive, 1994. http://classics.mit.edu/Plato/phaedrus.html.

————. *The Republic*. Translated by Benjamin Jowett. Salt Lake City, UT: Gutenberg Project, 2008. http://www.gutenberg.org/ebooks/1497.

Posner, George J., Kenneth A. Strike, Peter W. Hewson, and William A. Gertzog. "Accommodation of a Scientific Conception: Toward a Theory of Conceptual Change." *Science Education* 66, no. 2 (1982): 211–27. https://doi.org/10.1002/sce.3730660207.

Qiu, Linda. "17 Times Donald Trump Said One Thing and Then Denied It." *Politifact*, July 6, 2016. https://www.politifact.com/truth-o-meter/article/2016/jul/06/17-things-donald-trump-said-and-then-denied-saying/.

Qiu, Linda. "The Context Behind Trump's 'Animals' Comment." *New York Times*, May 18, 2018. https://www.nytimes.com/2018/05/18/us/politics/fact-check-trump-animals-immigration-ms13-sanctuary-cities.html.

Rasool, Amira. "Journalist Liz Plank Believes the Media Was Baited by Melania Trump's Zara Jacket." *Teen Vogue*, June 22, 2018. https://www.teenvogue.com/story/melania-trump-zara-jacket-gaslighting-media-liz-plank.

"Remarks by President Trump at a California Sanctuary State Roundtable." WhiteHouse.gov. May 16, 2018. https://www.whitehouse.gov/briefings-statements/remarks-president-trump-california-sanctuary-state-roundtable/.

Ricoeur, Paul. *On Translation*. Translated by Eileen Brennan. New York: Routledge, 2006.

————. "The Problem of Double Meaning as Hermeneutic Problem and as Semantic Problem." Translated by Kathleen McLaughlin. In *The Conflict* of *Interpretations: Essays in Hermeneutics*, edited by Don Hide, 62–78. Evanston, IL: Northwestern University Press, 1974.

Rocha, Samuel D. *Folk Phenomenology: Education, Study, and the Human Person.* Eugene, OR: Wipf and Stock, 2015.

———. *A Primer for Philosophy and Education.* Eugene, OR: Wipf and Stock, 2014.

Rogers, Katie, and Maggie Haberman. "Spotting CNN on a TV Aboard Air Force One, Trump Rages Against Reality." *New York Times*, July 24, 2018 (updated July 25, 2018). https://www.nytimes.com/2018/07/24/us/politics/trump-putin-cnn.html.

Rohn, Ulrike. "Lacuna or Universal? Introducing a New Model for Understanding Cross-cultural Audience Demand." *Media, Culture and Society* 33 (2011): 631–41. https://dx.doi.org/10.1177/0163443711399223.

Said, Edward. "Representing the Colonized: Anthropology's Interlocutors." *Critical Inquiry* 15 (1989): 205–25. https://www.jstor.org/stable/1343582.

Sapir, Edward. "The Status of Linguistics as a Science." *Language* 5 (1929): 207–14.

Saussure, Ferdinand de. *Cours de linguistique générale.* Paris: Payot, 1916.

———. *Course in General Linguistics.* Translated by Wade Baskin. New York: Philosophical Library, 1959.

Schudson, Michael, and Barbie Zelizer. "Fake News in Context." Paper prepared for "Understanding and Addressing the Disinformation Ecosystem," a workshop held at the Annenberg School for Communication, University of Pennsylvania, Philadelphia, December 15–16, 2017. In *Understanding and Addressing the Disinformation Ecosystem*, 1–4. https://firstdraftnews.org/wp-content/uploads/2018/03/The-Disinformation-Ecosystem-20180207-v4.pdf.

Scott, A. O. "Open Wide: Spoon-Fed Cinema." *New York Times*, August 7, 2009. https://www.nytimes.com/2009/08/09/movies/09scot.html.

Scranton, Roy. "'Star Wars' and the Fantasy of American Violence." *New York Times*, July 2, 2016. https://nyti.ms/29kM2ql.

Shannon, C. E. "A Mathematical Theory of Communication." *Bell System Technical Journal* 27 (1948): 379–423 and 623–56.

Shuessler, Jennifer. "With '1984' on Broadway, Thoughtcrime Hits the Big Time." *New York Times*, June 15, 2017. https://www.nytimes.com/2017/06/15/theater/with-1984-on-broadway-thoughtcrime-hits-the-big-time.html.

Sillen, Samuel. "Maggot-of-the-Month." In Howe, *Orwell's* Nineteen Eighty-Four, 297–99.

Simon, Scott. "Opinion: Calling the Press the Enemy of the People Is a Menacing Move." National Public Radio, August 4, 2018. https://www.npr.org/2018/08/04/635461307/opinion-calling-the-press-the-enemy-of-the-people-is-a-menacing-move.

Steiner, George. *After Babel: Aspects of Language and Translation.* 3rd ed. New York: Oxford University Press, 1998.

Stephens, Bret. "Trump, MS-13, and Fake News." *New York Times*, May 18, 2018. https://www.nytimes.com/2018/05/18/opinion/trump-ms13-fake-news.html.

———. "Trump Will Have Blood on His Hands." *New York Times*, August 3, 2018. https://www.nytimes.com/2018/08/03/opinion/trump-fake-news-enemy.html.

Stevens, Martine Danielle. "Ultradeep: A Critical Discourse Analysis of Fort McMurray and the Fires of Climate Change." Master's thesis, University of Ottawa, 2018. https://ruor.uottawa.ca/handle/10393/37572.

Striphas, Ted. "Communication as Translation." In *Communication as . . . : Perspectives on Theory*, edited by Gregory J. Shepherd, Jeffrey St. John, and Ted Striphas, 232–41. Thousand Oaks, CA: Sage, 2006.

Trump, Donald. "Here's Donald Trump's Presidential Announcement Speech." *Time*, June 16, 2015. http://time.com/3923128/donald-trump-announcement-speech/.

Tuchman, Gaye. "Objectivity as Strategic Ritual: An Examination of Newsmen's Notions of Objectivity." *American Journal of Sociology* 77, no. 4 (1972): 660–79.

Understanding and Addressing the Disinformation Ecosystem. A collection of short papers prepared for "Understanding and Addressing the Disinformation Ecosystem," a workshop held at the Annenberg School for Communication, University of Pennsylvania, December 15–16, 2017. https://firstdraftnews.org/wp-content/uploads/2018/03/The-Disinformation-Ecosystem-20180207-v4.pdf.

Uribe-Jongbloed, Enrique, and Hernán David Espinosa-Medina. "A Clearer Picture: Towards a New Framework for the Study of Cultural Transduction in Audiovisual Market Trades." *Observatorio* 8, no. 1 (2014): 23–48. http://obs.obercom.pt/index.php/obs/article/view/707.

Vološinov, V. N. *Marxism and the Philosophy of Language.* 1929. Translated by L. Matejka and I. R. Titunik. Cambridge, MA: Harvard University Press, 1986.

Vosoughi, Soroush, Deb Roy, and Sinan Aral. "The Spread of True and False News Online." *Science* 359 (2018): 1146–51. https://science.sciencemag.org/content/359/6380/1146.

Wachowski, Lana, and Lilly Wachowski, dirs. *The Matrix*. Los Angeles: Warner Brothers, 1999.

Walker, Craig Stewart. "Madness, Dissidence and Transduction." *Palabra Clave* 20, no. 3 (2017): 686–701. http://dx.doi.org/10.5294/pacla.2017.20.3.5.

Weaver, Warren. "The Mathematics of Communication." *Scientific American* 181, no. 1 (1949): 11–15.

Whorf, Benjamin Lee. "Science and Linguistics." *Technology Review* 42, no. 6 (1940): 229–31 and 247–48. http://web.mit.edu/allanmc/www/whorf.scienceandlinguistics.pdf.

Yagoda, Ben. "How Old Is 'Gaslighting'?" *Lingua Franca*, January 12, 2017. https://www.chronicle.com/blogs/linguafranca/2017/01/12/how-old-is-gaslight/

Index

Honduras, 108
Horkheimer, Max, 8–9
humanities, 15–16, 124, 131. *See also*
    social sciences
humour, 74, 120.

identity, 5, 42, 47, 100, 131
indexicals, 7
India, 50
inductive reasoning, 23, 45, 78,
    120–21. *See also* deductive
    reasoning; examples; jumping in
    (epistemological stance)
internet, 56, 96, 99–100
Internet Research Agency, 100
interpretants, 32–33, 83–85; and
    expansion of meaning, 37n15, 38,
    40, 43, 84; and frames, 84–85, 92,
    110; and *Nineteen Eighty-Four*,
    57, 59, 65. *See also* Peirce,
    Charles; semiotics
interpretive frames, 73–92, 94, 106,
    109–14. *See also* Peirce, Charles;
    semiotics
interpretive horizon, 17–18, 39. *See
    also* symbolic order
invention, 27, 41, 45–46, 75–80; and
    Petr Pavlenskii, 85; politics of,
    40–43, 124, 128; and translation,
    71, 80, 91–92. *See also* Aristotle;
    rhetoric
inverted pyramid, 98
Iraq, 20

jargon, 5, 121
Jefferson, Thomas, 62, 101
jokes. *See* humour
Jonientz, Joel, 19–20

journalism, 84n22, 94–95, 102, 105;
    and fake news, 99–100, 106–8,
    113–16; and objectivity, 96–99,
    103
jumping in (epistemological stance),
    xv, 23, 117–27, 131; and hunger,
    118

Kiev (Ukraine), 81, 87–88

legal system, 76, 83, 86–91, 98
logos, 77–78, 86n25. *See also*
    enthymeme; examples
London, 41, 51

Maitland, Sarah, 4n2, 6, 21n25. *See
    also* cultural translation
Marx, Karl, xv, 25, 30, 34. *See also*
    Grundrisse (book); materialism
materialism, 27, 29–34, 36, 38. *See
    also Grundrisse* (book); Marx,
    Karl
Matrix, The (film), 59–60
Mattelart, Armand, 129
meaning, 4–6, 20, 29–32, 34, 40,
    84; contested, 4, 32, 40–45, 105,
    120; evolution of, 94–95, 124;
    and jokes, 74–75; in *Nineteen
    Eighty-Four*, 52, 54–56, 65–66, 69;
    and power, 128. *See also* cultural
    translation; interpretants;
    polysemy; semantics; semiotics
Mercieca, Jennifer, 107
metacognition, xii
metatheory, xii, 23, 121, 125–26
method (in social sciences), 15,
    131n3
Mexico, 109

Mims, Margaret, 108, 110–12
misreading, 6–7, 21–22, 49, 120. *See
also* cultural translation; parallax
view
modernity, 3, 82
Morley, David, xiv
Moscow (Russia), 80–81
Muller, Heidi, xii, 129

National Public Radio, 99
Newspeak, 47–48, 52–53; affixes in,
55; contradictions of, 62–64;
and destruction of words, 54;
and duckspeak, 57; and Ingsoc,
53; philosophy of, 48, 56–58, 62,
vocabularies of, 53–54. See also
Nineteen Eighty-Four; Orwell,
George; solipsism
New York Times, 9, 74, 94, 99, 106,
109–16
n-gram, 101
Nineteen Eighty-Four (novel), 22,
47–72, 93–94, 115–16, 127; Big
Brother, 49, 51, 61, 68; the
Brotherhood, 50, 61, 64n21;
doublethink, 49, 51–54, 63–64,
67; Eastasia (place), 50, 61;
Eurasia (place), 50, 61; Inner
Party, 50; interpretations of,
51–52, 71n1, 94; Julia (character),
50, 65, 67–68; Ministry of Love,
50, 64; Ministry of Peace, 50;
Ministry of Plenty, 50; O'Brien
(character), 50–51, 57–60, 64,
66–69, 93; Oceania (place),
49–50, 53, 58, 60–61, 64; Outer
Party, 50; the Party, 49–50, 53,
57–58, 60–69, 127; proles, 50,

65, 68n22; and singing, 65–66,
68n22; Thought Police, 49, 65,
68n22; "We are the dead," 68;
and Winston Smith (character),
49–50, 54, 57–60, 64–69, 71,
93. *See also* Newspeak; Orwell,
George; solipsism
nonverbal signs, 63–66
Nowotny, Stefan, 42–43

objectivity, 94–99; and news, 96–98,
100, 103, 105–6; and philosophy,
96, 98. *See also* fake news;
subjectivity
Open University, xiii
Orwell, George, 22, 48–49, 51–52,
56, 62, 94, 121; *Animal Farm*
(book), 49; "Politics and the
English Language" (essay), 49,
52. *See also* Newspeak; *Nineteen
Eighty-Four*

Pakistan, 50
paralipsis, 107
parallax view, 7, 17–21, 122, 125; of
"Encoding/Decoding," 26, 45;
of *Nineteen Eighty-Four*, 48, 52;
strategies for inducing, 71, 80,
94. *See also* misreading
pathos, 77–78
Pavlenskii, Petr, 75–76, 80,
91–92, 94, 116, 121, 128; and
"actions," 75, 80–81, 84; and art
critics, 82–83; and "Freedom"
(*Свобода*), 81, 88–91; and
legal frame, 83, 87, 89–91; and
political frame, 86, 88; and

solipsism, 57–62; weak form, 71–72.
  See also Newspeak; *Nineteen
  Eighty-Four*
Solo, Han (fictional character), 18
South America, 50
Soviet Union, 50, 81
St. Étienne (France), 118–19
St. Petersburg (Russia), 80–81,
  87–88, 100
Star Wars (film franchise), 18, 20–21,
  38, 127
Steiner, George, 39–40
Stephens, Bret, 114
Stewart, Jon, 102
style, 8–9
subjectivity, 33–34, 36, 38, 82, 96. *See
  also* objectivity
Swift, Jonathan, 51
syllogisms, 39, 79, 85–88,
  90–91, 106, 109–11. *See also*
  enthymemes; Peirce, Charles
symbolic order, 72. *See also*
  interpretive horizon

technē, 14, 16, 124
telegraphy, 97
telephony, 26–28
television, 22, 30–34, 40, 117, 131
theory: axioms of, 14–16, 123–26;
  within communication studies,
  xii, 7, 15, 22–23, 26, 28, 117, 124–
  26; and pedagogy, xii–xiv, 13–14,
  17; within translation studies,
  26, 45–46, 120; trippiness
  of, 125. *See also* "Encoding/
  Decoding" (essay); humanities;
  jumping in (epistemological
  stance); metatheory;

sender-message-receiver model
  of communication; *technē*
translation. *See* axioms
translation studies, xiii, 7–8, 11–12,
  42, 53
Tuchman, Gaye, 98, 103, 106
Twitter, 100, 104, 107

UK Independence Party (British
  political party), 47
United States, 23, 42–43, 98, 102,
  115; 2016 presidential election,
  94, 102, 105; Declaration of
  Independence, 62; Immigration
  and Customs Enforcement,
  108–9

Veterans of Foreign Affairs, 106
Viennese Actionists, 82
Vološinov, V.N., 34

Weaver, Warren, 28–30, 32, 121. *See
  also* sender-message-receiver
  model of communication
Whorf, Benjamin Lee, 56–57. *See
  also* Sapir-Whorf hypothesis
Writing Culture (book), 4

Yasman, Pavel, 88–92

Zelizer, Barbie, 101, 105